Rich In All But Money
Life In Hungate 1900-38

by
Van Wilson

Revised edition 2007

York Archaeological Trust
Oral History Series: 1

This project is supported by the Garfield Weston Foundation

Designed and typeset by Lesley Collett, York Archaeological Trust

Printed by B & B Press, Rotherham

ISBN No. 978-1 874454 40 3

Contents

Hugh Bayley MP

HOUSE OF COMMONS
LONDON SW1A 0AA

This book is a vivid recollection of life in Hungate in the early years of the 20th century. The story is told by men and women who lived there – some in appalling conditions of squalor – who somehow managed to maintain pride in themselves, their homes and their community. They lived through a time of radical change. In his 1901 social survey of York, Seebohm Rowntree described Hungate as "one of the main slum districts of York". Fewer than half the houses had their own cold water tap. Forty years later the slums had been cleared and their inhabitants had moved to new council houses. One resident recalls the magic of moving into a council house with electric lights.

It is a story told by survivors. The narrators are well into retirement and some, sadly, have passed away. In 1900, one child in four died before their first birthday. By 1936 it was one child in thirteen. Now, in the 21st century, with the National Health Service, it is one in 175.

York generally has been very good at conserving its archaeology and historic buildings. This book, too, is a miracle of conservation – preserving ordinary citizens' memories of the past for future generations.

This revised edition has been published to link in with the new excavation of Hungate by York Archaeological Trust, the largest excavation in York for 25 years. There is a strong connection between oral history and archaeology. Both in their different ways tell us about past generations and their communities, helping us to understand our heritage.

I wish York Archaeological Trust every success as they work on this most important excavation, and am pleased to be associated with it.

Hugh Bayley MP

Preface

The original version of this book was published in February 1996. It came out of an oral history project run by York's Archaeological Resource Centre and the York Oral History Society covering the recent history of St Saviour's parish. The ARC (now called DIG) held an open day and invited residents and ex-residents of the parish to come and look around the old church of St Saviour's, where the ARC was based, and rekindle their memories of the area. Interested people were then interviewed in their own homes by volunteers.

From that beginning, stories were gathered and copies of the interviews held in the York Oral History Society archive. A picture of the area began to emerge and the result was an exhibition and a book on Hungate. This sold out in a few weeks and was reprinted in 1997.

Ten years later, York Archaeological Trust began a five-year dig on part of the Hungate site. With the demolition of some of the buildings facing onto Stonebow, the empty ground was ripe for excavation to begin. During the five years, there will be opportunities for the public to explore the site and see the results of the archaeological investigation, going back down the centuries from the 20th century to Roman times. It is a very important excavation, the biggest since the Coppergate dig over 25 years ago. During the excavation, more interviews will be carried out with people who worked in the area after 1938.

Profiles of Hungate Parish Residents

Mrs Louisa Aldrich

Born Louisa Grant in 1919 in Webster's Passage off St Saviourgate, Mrs Aldrich went to Castlegate School and remembers a great deal about domestic life in the Hungate area. She went into service after school, then to work at Armstrong Oilers on Lendal Bridge, and later worked for Woodcock's Bakers, doing much of the baking. During the Second World War, she was in the Women's Land Army.

Jack Birch

Born in 1911 in St Saviourgate, Mr Birch was familiar with the architecture and buildings of the district. He attended Fishergate School and then joined his father's building firm, rising to become Managing Director of William Birch & Sons. Mr Birch died a few years ago.

Harry Burnett

Mr Burnett was born in 1920 and, until his death in early 1995, lived in Clifton with his wife Joyce, who came originally from Haver Lane. He attended Park Grove School and went to Centenary Chapel.

Mrs Alice Butterworth

Born Alice Harris in 1906, Mrs Butterworth lived in Garden Street but is now a Clifton resident. She was a pupil of Castlegate School, and also regularly went to the Band of Hope and the Hungate Mission Sunday School. She remembers playing on Pound Garth and talks about local characters and about Leetham's Mill where her father worked.

James Cave

Mr Cave was born in 1910 in St Saviourgate, and attended the nearby Haughton School. His memory covers many subjects, and he was able to provide a wealth of detail about people and places.

Edward (Ted) Chittock

Mr Chittock, who in later years lived in Huntington, was born in Hungate, and was a member of the York Boys' Club, which trained some well-known boxers. Mr Chittock remembers local characters, pubs and housing conditions. He stresses the strong community spirit which existed in the area.

Mrs Dorothy Cook

Born Dorothy Barker in 1920, Mrs Cook lived in Hungate between the ages of five and thirteen. She went to Castlegate School, and later lived in Wigginton. She is the granddaughter of Mr and Mrs Barker, the Hungate undertaker and midwife.

Reg Deighton

Mr Deighton was born in 1925 and spent most of his childhood in St Andrewgate. He attended Bedern School and helped out at Clancy's rag and bone dealers. He remembers the chicory works on Layerthorpe and the local competitions for linnet singing.

Mrs Nell Fearn

Born Nellie Goodwin in 1918, the daughter of a tailor, Mrs Fearn lived in Dundas Street until the age of 17. She described the area as 'tough', yet at the same time a warm and caring community.

Mrs Cecelia Felton and Mrs Irene Thompson

Mrs Thompson was born Irene Thorpe in 1926, and her sister Cecelia in 1928, in Stonebow Lane. Their grandmother had a smallholding in Spen Lane, keeping goats and chickens, and their uncle raced whippets on Pound Garth. Their father, who served with the West Yorkshire Regiment in the First World War, played the piano in the Woolpack.

Mrs May Greenley

Born May Fearn in 1909, Mrs Greenley spent many years in Spen Lane and remembers being poor but happy. Her family attended St Saviour's Church and her mother took in theatrical lodgers. May herself once danced in the chorus at the Empire but was not allowed to continue there and had to go to work at Terry's.

Mr and Mrs Hall
Joseph (known as Stan) Hall was born in Broom's Court, Hungate, in 1911, and Mrs Lily Hall in Sawmill Lane, Hungate, in 1912. They married in 1935 and moved to live in the Groves. They talk about children's games, about friends, work and life in the 1920s and 30s.

Walter Holmes
Wally Holmes was born in 1925 in Dundas Street, and moved to Clifton later on. He remembers the popular Woolpack rugby team, and the many local tradesmen, bringing their goods by horse and cart. He talks about the Gas Company, the Electric Cinema and the pawnbrokers.

Mrs Lavinia Kay
Born Lavinia Lawson in St John's Place, Hungate, in 1925, Mrs Kay went to Bedern School and played on Pound Garth. She remembers the appalling conditions in which families had to live, and the colourful characters of the time.

Mrs Valerie Law
Valerie Shirbon lived at the sweet shop on the corner of St Saviourgate from the 1940s to 1960s before moving to Fulford. She helped in her mother's shop and met many of the local residents.

Mrs Dorothy Reynolds and her son Guy King-Reynolds
Mrs Reynolds was born Dorothy Baker in 1903 and became the wife of Dr Reynolds at 18 St Saviourgate. Her son, Mr King-Reynolds, lives in Bath. They describe living conditions, poverty and health in this area, and tell how Dr Reynolds was the first Labour councillor for the Guildhall Ward.

Mrs Rene Sheard

Mary Irene (Rene) Wright was born in the Black Swan, Peasholme Green, in 1911, and then moved across the road to the Woolpack where her father was landlord. She attended the Haughton School and Sunday School at St Saviour's. She died in March 1995.

George Squire

Mr Squire was born in 1925 in Haver Lane, and later lived in a greengrocer's in Carmelite Street. He moved to Strensall and became a Master Builder. He remembers how everything seemed dark and grey compared to modern times, and yet it was a very sociable, 'self-help' community.

Mrs Violet Taylor

Born in 1906 in Darlington, Violet came to York at the age of six months. Her father took the Leeds Arms in Hungate. Although he died in 1918, Violet's mother, Charlotte Pritchard, continued to run the pub for another 20 years, with the help of her children including Violet.

Samuel Thompson

Mr Thompson was baptised at St Saviour's Church in 1921, where his parents had earlier been married. He was the middle one of six children, attended Castlegate and Bedern schools and worked at Rowntree's for almost 50 years.

John Waite

Mr Waite was born at 3 St Saviour's Place in 1923, the middle one of three children. His mother lived in that house from the 1880s to her death in 1957. His father was a pork butcher.

Arnold (Andy) Waudby

Andy Waudby was born in Hungate in 1921 and as an adult lived in Upper Poppleton. He remembers the street games, a popular feature of childhood, and has made modern-day equivalents, such as a wooden rack for playing marbles. Andy had part-time jobs from the age of ten, always managing to find ways to make a bit of money, such as delivering fruit and vegetables and singing outside the pubs.

Ernest Webster

Mr Webster was born in Duke of York Street in 1901, and was a Blue Coat schoolboy. Despite the strict discipline he endured, he learnt many useful crafts there and afterwards entered into apprenticeship.

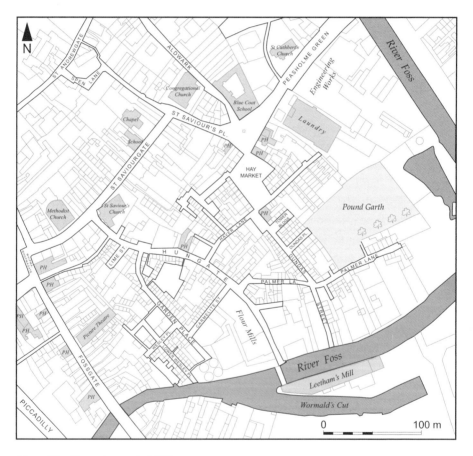

Map of the Hungate area in 1936

Reproduced from the 1936 Ordnance Survey map with the kind permission of the Ordnance Survey

Chapter 1

The Environment

In the early part of the twentieth century, the Hungate district was one of the poorest in York, and was likened to a rabbit warren, because so many houses were packed into such a small space. The inhabitants were victim to the dirt and grime of local industry, as well as the vile smells from slaughterhouses and chicory works. Their homes were dwarfed by the huge prison-like building of Leetham's Mill, which stood on the promontory of the Foss and dominated the skyline. The streets were subject to flooding and the houses in such a terrible state that eventually they had to be demolished in the 1930s.

Bradleys Buildings, Hungate, 1911

Yet despite poverty, disease and deprivation, or perhaps because of these common enemies, the people who lived in the area testify to a strong community spirit, where neighbours cared about each other and shared what little they had. Often those who suffer together and share adversity have stronger connections than those who are more secure.

When the residents were relocated to spanking new council houses in Clifton, Tang Hall and other parts of the city, seeing electric lighting, bathrooms and indoor toilets for the first time, many of them still missed the old way of life. They longed for the sharing and the comradeship, and many of them felt that this was lost for ever when Hungate was torn down.

The Parish

The parish itself formed roughly the shape of a square, bordering Aldwark, St Saviourgate, (a rather more affluent street, though the many courts and yards which led off it were the opposite), part of Fossgate and the River Foss.

Jack Birch sets the scene:

Stonebow as it exists at present was simply not there. To get from Pavement to Heworth, the main road was St Saviourgate, then approaching the end, you turned right into St Saviour's Place, then Peasholme Green.

The land to the south of St Saviourgate was approached two ways. From Peasholme Green, where there was a fairly large open area known as the Haymarket, or by Hungate. Apart from the industrial complex on the River Foss, of Leetham's Mill, the rest of the area was full of run-down houses.

According to Samuel Thompson,

As you came down Hungate, near St Saviour's Church, where the garage is, underneath there was supposed to be a passage through to York Minster. And I've actually stood there. I could take you to it now.

Mr Deighton remembers the transport.
The trams used to come down Whip-ma-whop-ma-gate, up St Saviourgate. Then they had buses. They used to call 'em trackless, because they was the same as trams but without the tracks. They was navy blue and white, run by the corporation. They used to run by overhead electricity but they could steer where they wanted. The electrobus had a battery in it, it had to be charged up.

Andy Waudby evokes the familiar smells of the area.

*You had this mist off the river, and the smell was like chickweed. If
you go to a stagnant pond anywhere you can smell it. I recognise it
as soon as I smell it. Hungate. And then where Dan Parkin had his
'osses, so you got the smell off the manure heap. Now to clean the
drains out, the corporation used to bring a two wheeled cart down.
And you had the blokes with big poles, with a box on the end, and they
used to lift the grate up and scoop all the muck out into this thing.
Now in summer the smell from those drains, it was like midnight in
the Shambles. Talk about Eau de Cologne. Then you had the smell from
the slaughterhouses. And you had the smoke and the smell from the
gasworks. Everybody was affected because when you had a foggy day
you'd get smoke from all the chimleys.*

*On a Saturday you'd get this water tank on two wheels, and a
corporation bloke used to come with the 'oss and this tank, and pull a
lever and at back there was like a pipe of water, a stream to keep the dust
down. You could get more water by spitting on it.*

Not all the houses in the parish were the same. The beauty and
comparative grandeur of St Saviourgate contrasted sharply with the
run-down tenements of Bedern. Reg Deighton describes Ebor Buildings
in Bedern.

*These was tenement flats, with a common staircase that used to be open
at every floor and they used to live off them. And the kids that lived
there were really down and out. They used to come to school with their
shoes fastened round the neck and they only put the shoes on when they
got to school, because Mr Cammidge wouldn't allow 'em into the school
without shoes on.*

*There was only two rooms in some of them. And they was five or six
kids to a family. But I can never remember any nastiness with the*

people in Bedern who were just poor, out of work, and through being out of work they was on the breadline. But you go round the corner into Aldwark and the people there all had good jobs. They worked at the railway, corporation, and the brewery which was down there.

Nell Fearn also remembers Ebor Buildings.

It was like in these old American films, the tenements. I had a friend that went to our school, that used to live in there and she was off ill. They asked me to call in and see her to find out what was matter with her. It was like being in a maze. I got frightened in the finish. I'd be about ten then. There was prams and cats and dogs, and rabbit hutches with rabbits in, on the landings. And I never found her.

Hungate was self-contained. You knew exactly where you were, no matter what alleyway you went in, what doorway you went through. And eventually all you did was come out of it into Fossgate or Pavement.

Ted Chittock recalls the different types of housing.

My sister lived in a garret where the steps was probably two feet across. And it spiralled up stone steps, up and off the landings was the rooms. And all those consisted of one room. Then there was St John's Place where I was born and that was off Haver Lane. Now those was the normal two up two down. The floor was quarry tiles. There was a front room and a back kitchen. The staircase led to the bedrooms. The fireplace was where you did all the cooking. It was a big black range with the old spit over the top of it.

Then you had a contrast across the road in St Saviourgate, where me sister moved into some years later, which was a big house, with a Georgian frontage and a balustraded staircase. There was the doctors like Reynolds down there, and he was a very good doctor, because once I had an accident on Centenary Chapel. I stuck a spike in me leg and we went across to Reynolds and fixed it.

Brass Rapper Row [Carmelite Street] *was a famous place, where all the row of houses had brass rappers. Every woman on a morning used to stone the steps. That's how proud they were of their homes. There was a house in Hungate what had a tree growing up through the front room – believe it or not.*

When they started pulling it down, they found a mysterious room, people had been complaining about for years, where there was knocking going on. And when they opened this room, it had obviously been an undertaker's. There was a cart in it, old chisels, and half-made coffins stuck up on the walls.

A similar story to this has come from several people. Apparently when buildings were being demolished in the 1930s, there was one workshop which was locked. The authorities eventually traced the very elderly gentleman who had the key, and the place was opened. Inside there was a workbench with part of a coach on the bench, a coat hanging up on the door, a cup with the dregs of what had once been tea, and a calendar with the year 1917. A mystery to rival the Marie Celeste! One possible explanation is that the workman had been called up suddenly and left for the war, never to return.

Mrs Reynolds lived in St Saviourgate but visited Bedern.

There was a passageway called Kendal's Passage and down the passage were lots of little cottages, and Mr Kendal used to come every morning, a very big man, very tall, and he always wore a high hat and tails. One of the old school! And all these cottages belonged to him.

These places shared a pump in the middle of the yard, and this is where you'd see the little kids standing at the end, very often in bare feet.

In Bedern, the places were absolutely terrible and they belonged to an
alderman, and we were horrified to think that he lived in such opulence
and these poor things...I can remember my husband [Dr Reynolds]
telling me, "Darling, you can't possibly be a Conservative when things
are like that...you must come with me and I'll show you", and he took
me round.

There was buckets of urine and everything else on the landings. There
were no lavatories. Bare stairs too, I can remember that. No-one
believed they lived in such a terrible state and I must say the people
were really charming although they were suffering such poverty. In the
olden days, York was known as the three P's – poor, proud and pretty.
Under the pretty side was the seamy side.

*Toilet block excavated by York Archaeological Trust during the redevelopment of the Hungate
area, 2007*

Rene Sheard remembers,

*Off Haymarket there was a square of houses which went round into
Brunswick Terrace. It was a big square, there was about twelve houses*

and they shared a communal yard at the back with one solitary grate for the slops. All these twelve houses, all the slops went down there and I think there was about half a dozen toilets at the very end of the yard.

In 1912, the Medical Officer of Health decided that some houses on Brunswick Terrace should be demolished. He inspected on 9th July, and again on the 11th. He served a closing order on 25th September, with a notice to quit on 13th December. A demolition order was served on 13th February 1913. Although the landlord wanted to make improvements, the Health Officer stated that 'it cannot possibly be rendered fit for human habitation'.

Mrs Sheard also recalls Haver Lane. Part of this street was excavated in the 2007 Hungate dig.

It was a very narrow little street. Tiny footpath at either side, and the families seemed to be brought up on the footpaths. In summer all the children were outside because the little places they lived in were too small for 'em. They'd be overcrowded inside. But there always seemed to be crowds of children on the footpaths.

Left: Archaeologists uncover the surface of Haver Lane in excavations in 2007
Right: Haver Lane as it was in about 1933

John Waite lived in St Saviourgate, but he related well to the Hungate children.

Compared to Hungate houses, ours was a decent house. But all my friends were down in Hungate, where I played with them, which is why I know so many of them from Hungate.

Ours was a big house but there was no electricity. Even until 1958 it was gas, and there was only two rooms where you had a gas mantle. The other rooms had open gas, a flame which stuck up like the fingers of your hand, blue flames and yellow flames, naked light. It was a three storey house and a cellar down below. There was a big kitchen to the back with a boiler, an open fire for oven cooking and hot water. It was people who had money who had it built in the first place, because in the passage there was about four or five bells on a coiled spring, and then in the room beside the fireplace, you had a little ebony black knob you used to pull and it would ring one of these bells for the servants to come.

It was bombed in the First World War, and my mother's eye was cut. A lady over the road lost her eye, and there was a man killed outside at the time. And if you look at the house today, you'll find at the front it's new brick work. A Zeppelin it was in them days.

He has good cause to remember the cellar particularly.

The coal cellar had a little iron grate just before the step, where the coalman used to throw his coal down the chute. Sometimes if we were really bad, my father would shove us down there, and it was a black, frightening place to go down. One day I got sick of being down there and frightened to death, so I climbed up the coal chute, and it was coming dusk. A neighbour from round the corner, she and her husband were coming by and she got the fright of her life. She hit her husband with her handbag because he did nothing to help her, and her money fell out and he ran away and she ran after him. In putting my hand across

I got the feel of a bit of money, and I was as black as the ace of spades when I came in at night. But my mother protected us before my father came in, otherwise I'd have got a good hiding.

Floods in Lower Wesley Place, 1933

The Streets

Constant floods made the houses damp and there were rats, as Reg Deighton observes.

Talk about rats – whether they were water voles or not I don't know. But it was fair game for fellers to go ratting with the terriers on a Sunday morning, and have bets. For every rat caught you got a penny. Everybody used to have a little terrier or a whippet.

*Going down Layerthorpe, all those yards go down to the Foss.
Whenever the Ouse used to flood, the Foss used to flood. And they all
used to get covered in three or four feet of water in the houses.*

Mrs Butterworth remembers the water coming very close.

*It used to come up Garden Place. It's just high enough to get into the
rooms. We were standing on duckboards. We used to have about four
gas lamps in Garden Place.*

Garden Place, 1930s

There were some advantages to the floods as Nell Fearn discovered.

*Walker's coal yard was on Layerthorpe Bridge. It used to wash the coal
out, and it used to come down in the water, and as it came past the*

bottom of Dundas Street, where the railings were, pieces used to come in through the railings, battered about, so you were sent out with a bucket and your bare feet. You didn't have wellies in those days. And you used to go collecting coal and take it back, and dry 'em in front of the fire.

Although the floods left behind a terrible mess, the housewives still kept the streets as clean as they could, as Lavinia Kay points out.

Stonebow Lane, which connected Hungate with Whip-ma-whop-ma-gate, was a yard wide. We had road-sweepers, but our mothers used to have us scrubbing the pavement and the stone. You coloured your own steps. You did the part of your pavement where you lived, which was your little responsibility.

Alice Butterworth's family was certainly house-proud.

Our yard was tarmac, but it was all broke, and we used to sweep it and then stone round the cement round grates. With it being flats, it went up a passage, and there was two lots of stairs, one lot for your second floor and one lot for the third and we used to stone the passage, make it nice and clean. There was never any rubbish knocking around like there is today. Always nice and clean curtains up, lace curtains.

Harry Burnett's family was proud too.

All you had was a big floor but it was spotlessly clean because the women used to get on their hands and knees and scrub it like hell. You could guarantee all the doorsteps in Garden Place and Hungate was always highly scrubbed, with carbolic soap and a brush.

Of course the streets had gas lamps and John Waite describes how they were lit.

At the end of St. Saviourgate now, it used to be Salem Chapel, and over in the corner there was a red pillar box, and a gas lamp, and the old lamplighter used to come on his big bicycle and a pole over his shoulder. He'd cycle down there, and he'd click it and the light would go on, and then in the morning he'd come and put this little cap over the top of it, to put it out, then put the pole on his back and cycle off. They were that good, many a time they didn't even stop, they used to just come slowly by and do it.

The Houses

In 1885 a Royal Commission was held and the result was that the 1890 Housing of the Working Classes Act was passed. Local councils were given responsibility to improve housing in their areas. Over the next years, council estates began to appear but it was a slow process. The York Health Office did extensive surveys in the Hungate area in 1907, and found many properties 'unfit for human habitation'. They identified 201 properties as 'unhealthy' – 10 in Bellerby's Yard, 5 in Black Horse Passage, 10 in Bradley's Buildings, 3 in Brenton Place, 6 in Brunswick Place, 7 in Carmelite Street, 6 in Church Buildings, 5 in Clark's Yard, 4 in Drummond's Court, 15 in Dundas Street, 4 in Foster's Yard, 15 in Garden Place, 5 in tenements off Garden Place,18 in Haver Lane, 18 in Hungate, 2 in Leadley's Cottages, 6 in Leadley's Yard, 2 in Lime Street, 8 in Lower Dundas Street, 5 in Lower Wesley Place, 7 in Oglesby's Court, 5 in Palmer Lane, 7 in Sawmill Lane, 1 in Senior's Yard, 11 in St John's Place, 5 in Towler's Buildings, 7 in Wesley Place and 4 in Wide Yard.

There were also houses in Peasholme Green. For example, number 5 was a small terraced property housing two adults and four children under ten. The house had one bedroom. The kitchen had very damp walls, the pointing on the front walls was found to be defective, there was no proper ashbin and they had to use a trough w.c. in the yard. The rent was three shillings a week, which was quite a lot for the time.

The shoemaker's shop at number 4 was also damp, with dirty walls and defective floors with missing tiles. Number 6 was even worse, housing two adults and three children under ten. The kitchen walls were very damp, the bottom of the fire-grate broken, the wall above the fireplace defective, the staircase defective, the back walls dilapidated, the pointing very bad and tiles on the kitchen floor broken. The front window would not open, there was no pantry, and the family had to use a trough w.c. in the yard. We talk about appalling conditions now but these are mind-boggling.

Five years later in 1912, the York Medical Officer of Health reported on numbers 16, 17, 18, 19 Dundas Street and 19 Palmer Lane, all owned by the same person. The houses were 'very closed in and ill lighted at the backs', there were very small windows to the sculleries and back bedrooms, and only three water closets for five houses. They had defective roofs, defective floors, windows which did not open properly, and external walls which required pointing to remedy the dampness. There were no proper ashbins, and no places to properly store food. In May 1913, the Town Clerk gave the owner a closing order on these houses, as they were 'in a state so dangerous or injurious to health as to be unfit for human habitation'. Orders on properties that year included houses in Brunswick Place, Carmelite Street, Cross Wesley Place, Dundas Street, Garden Place, Haver Lane, Haymarket, Hungate, Leadley's Yard, St John's Place and Wesley Place. Six houses in Lower Dundas Street were found to be very damp, dark and not properly ventilated, yet the rent was 2/6d. The kitchen floors had to be relaid with red tiles on a bed of cement concrete. There were repairs needed on woodwork, doors, floors, ceilings, plasterwork, fireplaces, window-sills, staircases, balustrades and fastenings. There were still privies and a joint ashpit and these had to be 'abolished' and a water closet provided. The drains had to be 'made to be smoke-tight, properly disconnected from the sewer and where they passed under the houses, embedded and surrounded with cement concrete six inches thick'. The kitchen sinks and the wet and defective plaster needed replacing, and all external walls, roofs and chimney stacks repointing.

It was really after the First World War that the process of improvement accelerated, when 'the poor physical health and condition of many urban recruits to the army was noted with shock and alarm'. The 1919 campaign 'Homes Fit for Heroes' resulted in the government subsidising the new council housing, though it was a few more years before this became widespread in York.

Mrs Alice Butterworth describes her house in Garden Street.

There was just two rooms and one was a kitchen. Toilet was outside. It was all rented down there. I don't think anybody had their own place. Well I think ours was about the only flats there was. And they did belong to Leetham's Mill. Everybody was overcrowded. There was ten of us, and we used to have two bedrooms in there so me mother had to partition it off with curtains.

Mrs Alice Butterworth, 1995

*Alice Butterworth
and her husband in
Garden Street, 1923*

She tells of how the families took pride in their homes, making sure they looked as neat and tidy as possible.

We had a lovely big York range. Could see yourself through it, blackleaded. Me dad used to do that. And we used to have a steel fender, and all stone floors. Bedroom was concrete. Kitchen was concrete,

25

used to do clip carpets did me dad. But we had our own tap in the back kitchen. Some people had pumps, some had taps in the courtyard.

My mother always had a gas stove. But she just used that in summer time when she didn't want a fire on. She always baked in a fire oven, and she'd maybe do a stew on the fire. But she wouldn't fry on it. She used to fry on her stove. Then summer time to save your coal for winter, used to use your gas stove.

Stan Hall emphasises the same pride, despite the struggle to survive.

My dad died in France five days after the war started. There was seven of us children and we lived in two up, two down, and one little back yard. And we had gas in our kitchen, little gas cooker. We got chance to go further away, it was two houses knocked into one, with four bedrooms. We had a great big yard but in that yard there was ever so many houses that had been half demolished and course there was no-one in them. But we had to go outside to our toilet and you had to take a light, it was so dark. For all them little houses were small, some of them were little palaces. Brass fenders, brass spittoons, everything brass.

Wally Holmes's mother, like most of the women, worked very hard to look after her family.

She used to go down [to the market] at eight o'clock Saturday night. We'd go as well, under the vegetable stalls, stuffing stuff into bags, vegetables, fruit and everything else there. Mother would get a piece of meat, weighed about two stone at least and that was our Sunday joint. And then sandwiches right up to Thursday the following week. And how they kept stuff fresh I don't know, but you did, because all that was over it was a small meshed net.

We were rich in everything else, and everybody mixed and kept together. Mother had to come home from market last thing and then

Garden Court in Hungate in about 1933. These houses were demolished in the late 1930s.

after that she'd set off and mix the dough. Big earthenware dish, then she'd put the cloth over it and leave it in the fireplace all night, on the Yorkish range. It'd stop there all night to ferment. Then she must have got up at least eight o'clock on Sunday morning, cos when we got up, our back yard was absolutely full of bread cakes, bread rolls and the smell of fresh bread and we had warm bread cakes for breakfast. We looked forward to that.

I'll never forget me mother one time and it stands out in my mind. She were baking and mixing and this was summertime and some caraway seed had got into the dough and whether it were one of us that knocked it into it or what, but me mother carried the whole lot, a big hunk of it, down to the Foss and heaved it over the edge.

Lavinia Kay recalls her house:

We had the old horse-hair sofa, old rocking chair, a chest of drawers and it was bow-fronted, and it had four big drawers and two little ones. We had a sideboard and then in the kitchen it was just a table and chairs. There was a coal fire in the front, with gas lighting, lots and lots of ornaments. I remember once me mother opened a drawer and it was absolutely full, running all over the place with black beetles. But we kept a dog and a cat.

Down Hungate you went down a kind of passage and it opened out into a square, and there were communal toilets and a big standpipe in the middle, like a concrete pillar with just one tap. And I would say about 15 houses shared that one tap. I think they were paved round the houses and cobbled stones in the middle.

Andy Waudby's house was similar.

The women used to scrub the steps. They would perhaps put pottery mould on the steps, like a bar of soap and you rub it on and it comes out purple white.

Then you used to get like a yellow block, like limestone, and rub that on. I used to ask why they always scrubbed the steps, and I learnt that it was to keep the devil away. And that's where it originated from.

Now a lot of houses in Hungate, you could walk right off the street into the house. You'd have a chest of drawers, a table in the middle, and a sofy. On the mantelpiece you'd get pot dogs or pot horses. Then the old range. You'd have a piece of material on the mantelpiece, hanging down with fringes, tassels on sometimes. Then candlesticks and ornaments.

My grandmother used to polish them every Friday.

Gaslighting was in the centre of the room. Now being poor, you're lucky if you could afford a mantle. It was like a piece of netting. And you put it on very gently, turn it to the right a little bit on two lugs. And this held it up. Then you'd get a match and light it and it used to flare up, and then it would go black a little bit, like sooty. And then it got hotter and hotter. Once you'd lit it, you just had to touch it or knock it, once you got hold of it, it just disintegrated.

Upstairs, you'd got a brass bedstead. Metal struts each side of the bed. So we've got brass on top and a brass end with railings and brass knobs on. That's where you got the saying 'with brass knobs on'.

Then we had a mattress, full of straw, about six inches wide. It was a good flea breeder, bug breeder. Then you had your sheets, if you were lucky you had sheets, if not you had a blanket. You couldn't afford a mantle upstairs, so all you had was a gas jet. Candles were good for burning fleas, especially bugs, cremate 'em. And then you'd have a washing stand with a wash bowl stuck in it. Nearly all the houses had a big jug and a bowl. They were small rooms, you couldn't swing a cat about in 'em.

So you'd have the women all helping the little ones. They'd be sat there eating on the stairs and as they got older, they go higher up the stairs. Time and time again you'd go into houses where a little lass or a lad had died of meningitis, it's nothing fresh to go in t'room and see a coffin on the clean tablecloth.

You always smelt of carbolic soap. The women's clothes were clean, the children were clean. Clean at morning, but by teatime looked as if they'd been up the bloody chimney. But I think to meself the womenfolk, they had a lot on their plate. Must have been a hard life, as hard as it was for the men in the flour mills and gasworks.

Mrs Thompson recalls that,

Nearly all houses was just an up and a down and one bedroom. You was lucky if you had two. And the toilets was duckets. I mean you could have gone through your own door to the toilet, but you could have shook hands with one in the one next to you, cos it was a long line went along. Toilet paper was newspaper torn up into squares and fastened on with a bit of string. No fancy stuff for us.

Reg Deighton's brother,

Used to live down Brunswick Place and he used to have two rooms upstairs and two down. Shared a toilet with another ten houses. The yard was so slippery with throwing soap water down and it used to go into one drain, the suds. It was like a layer of soap and I stood on it. Whoosh! Straight across the yard and banged me head, cried for a week.

Some houses had a 'best room' like Dorothy Cook's.

We had a front parlour used on special occasions, red plush, chesterfield and chairs. One with horsehair was in the living room. Dad used to play piano and there was a big aspidistra.

Louisa Aldrich lived in Webster's Passage:

There was no back way, there was just a front entrance, and it was a very long living room and adjoining that was another room, where you did cooking and that. Then adjoining that was what we used to call the Far Spot. It was all in one, one length.

And there was really plenty of room in it, but no facilities at all, but we had a coal fire which we did baking on. There wasn't hot and cold water.

*Mrs Nellie Fearn, 1995, and
(right) as Nellie Goodwin,
Dundas Street, 1934*

*I used to bake for my mother from maybe 12 years old, used to help her.
We had a fire cooker. Bars was in t'middle, then there was a little ledge
either side where you could put your pans. It was really a queer looking
oven, used to open out more like a range.*

Nell Fearn recalls that her family

Had the one living room/kitchen off Dundas Street, and a little kitchen at the back of that, and a little backyard. We had a copper, father used to burn anything. It was like being on an Indian reservation when he used to want to get it going in winter. There was a couple of taps in the middle so everybody used to go out and get their water from the middle there.

You're straight in and up the stairs, then you were straight into your living room. A nice big fireplace and a mantlepiece, tassels on your cover over the mantle. And always a fender, stainless steel, and a Tidy Betty which was a thing that went in front of the fire itself, so the ashes wouldn't come out onto the hearth.

Then there was your fire and this just went round in front, it had to be well brassed and everything, and an oven at the side of the fire. Used to have a big pan that you used to boil your washing in, on the top of the fire. Sheets and pillow cases and things like that, were boiled in that pan.

That was all in the one room, and there was another door you went in and we'd a little tiny kitchen, and there was a sink in there, a stone sink, and nothing else. We eventually had a gas cooker put in there.

May Greenley lived in

A little two bedroomed house in Spen Lane. Five of us kids and me mam, who was 28, lived there. We shared a toilet with next door, at end of the yard, and had to take buckets to put water down. Mother had to work any way she could, she did ironing for Dr Reynolds, ironed his shirts, and cleaned at Ross's fish shops. We had to sleep four girls in one room and the lad in the other and me mam on the sofa.

Used to clean up in the evenings. Mother made us all brush our hair for a long time. Friday night was paraffin night in case of nits, we put it on and then washed it off.

George Squire and his grandfather, Haver Lane, 1927, and (inset) George Squire with his grandfather's watch in 1995

Not only were the houses small but the area itself was gloomy as George Squire explains.

The living conditions were very bare. I remember them putting electric light in the shop on Carmelite Street. There was one cold tap and if you wanted water to get a bath, you used to boil it. You used to sit in the short bath on a Friday night in the front room. Everybody got bathed, and used the same water. In the terrace you had two bedrooms upstairs and one fire in the house, and that was the range. When you went to bed you bloody froze. You never slept in the sheet, you got in the blanket because the blanket was warm. The floors were flagged, we had pricked rugs in front of the fire. If they were all out I used to get a cat out of the street and catch mice cos the whole place was running with mice and there were rats outside with it being a mill. Used to see 'em in the corners where rubbish had been dumped.

We had ordinary chairs and settee when we had the shop. Dad bought it for half a crown and covered it himself with imitation leather. And a sideboard and a Marconi radio. Life was dreadfully hard in the 30s. It was very grey and drab everywhere, nothing in the streets. You'd see people on bikes and there was one car that came in Haver Lane and that was my uncle Charlie. He had an open top Chevy with a running board like Al Capone.

You never saw flowers. Bats used to fly around by gaslight. Everything was grey and dark, nothing bright. You never saw white shirts, always striped thick stuff, flannelette with no collars, flat caps and scarf round the necks. My grandfather had a Homburg. The men wore working boots but my Dad used to wear shoes.

The only clothes you had were two pairs of trousers, a vest, a shirt and a coat, a pair of boots or shoes or if things were bad, black plimsolls. We paid something every week.

But I think the worst thing of all were the blackclocks [black beetles]. *When you turned the light out and if you come round and struck a match, the floor would be covered in blackclocks. And you could smell them.*

St Saviourgate was very different from the poorer areas of the parish, and James Cave's home was in that street.

Our house was in a block of four and at the top of the last storey was attics, divided into two on one side of the house and two on the other, and you go through from one attic to the other because it sloped right back. My bedroom was in the attic on the top floor. Cats used to walk along the tiles. There was five flights of stairs, and cellars underneath it. The coal people used to come and on the pavement there used to be a square piece of iron on a chain, and they used to lift it up, empty the bags of coal in the main street, and put it back again.

My father was manager of an advertising business called Sheldon's, and they had the bottom floor as offices and workshops. Had eleven rooms in the house and one room called the best room upstairs. On either side of the fireplace you pulled levers and a bell rang in the passageway.

Valerie Law lived in a shop in St Saviourgate during the late 1940s and 50s.

Ours was a Georgian house with a cellar, ground floor, first floor, second floor and attic. Lovely big rooms and an old staircase. We used to run up and down and slide down banisters. The back yard was on two levels, full of flowers. Mum bought flowers every Saturday in the market. She put them into any kind of container she could find, and into the garden. We didn't have a back entrance so dustbins had to come through the house on Friday mornings.

When we first went there was a great big fireplace with black leading, brass handles and an oven at the side. It was in for two or three years, we didn't use it for cooking, but put our pyjamas in there at night to warm them ready for bed. One day, the door was open and the cat got in and when we opened it to put pyjamas in, it shot out. Fortunately it was all right. There was a door at the side of the fire which led to a little room under the stairs with a sloping roof, we put washing on clothes horses in there to dry.

Further down the street on the same side as the church there was a lovely double-fronted house. The daughter had a pony and kept it in the garden until she found somewhere to keep it. She had to take the pony through the house for about a month. There was an enormous garden with tennis court and vegetable plot, rose arches and a big lawn.

We all had our own jobs. On a Saturday I used to start at the top of the house and dust and polish all the way down. The sitting room wasn't used that often and one Sunday it smelt damp so I put the electric fire on, to leave it on for a couple of hours, and closed the door and forgot about it. The following Sunday when I worked my way down and opened the sitting room door, the heat just hit me. The electric fire had been left on the whole week! I daren't tell Mum but I plucked up courage to tell her, and all she said was, "Never mind, it's had a good airing".

Jack Birch also lived in the same street, yet he did not escape some of the problems which affected those in Hungate itself.

Jack Birch, 1995

Number 29 is a tall Georgian house. My father was very fond of it cos I remember the first floor, it was taken up by a drawing room, parallel with the street, which had a rather ornate cornice in it. Being a Georgian building there were lots of nooks and crannies, and I remember my mother was very disturbed because we had a plague of blackclocks – rain beetles.

You know they're about an inch in length. And we had a special gadget to trap these beasts. It was a type of open bowl in the centre of which was a small cup which held a liquid to attract the beetles. They proceeded to come up the sides of this apparatus, and when they got onto the portion of rods that supported the centre-piece, there was a two-sided flap and if they got slightly out of balance, this tipped and dropped the beetles into some poisonous liquid in the bowl. Mother used to catch large numbers of beetles that way.

Today St Saviourgate is not very different from its earlier self, but much of the surrounding area was condemned and had to be demolished between 1933 and 1938. A great many houses were razed to the ground and their inhabitants rehoused. One lady remembers that

When Hungate was taken down, there were so many rats around that the Corporation shovelled them onto carts to be taken away and gassed.

Stonebow, a wide street built in 1960, cut Hungate in two. Stonebow House, most of which is a multi-storey car park, is widely considered to be York's ugliest building.

When families were moved to new housing in Clifton, Tang Hall and other parts of the city, it was quite an upheaval. To begin with, all the houses' contents had to be removed, as Samuel Thompson witnessed.

In them days they used to bring a big van and put all your furniture in it and what they call fumigate it, to get rid of all the bugs. They took all

the stuff on a night time in this van. Everybody had these bugs, it was no good trying to say you hadn't.

Ted Chittock continues the story.

Then they took it to Foss Islands and they connected it up and they fumigated the whole of that van. So that when you went into your new house there was no danger of anything.

The difference between Hungate and the new council houses was enormous. Lavinia Kay recalls moving to a house in Peterhill Drive.

And we just had nothing, and we just had to wait while the van came. What I remember is we all got into trouble because when we'd got light bulbs we all went mad, running round and round putting switches on. My mother said, "If you don't leave them alone, it's gonna cost me money".

For many residents the move was a traumatic experience, which took years to come to terms with. Perhaps some never have. Alice Butterworth echoes many others when she says,

Wish I was there now. I do. I wish I lived there now.

Chapter 2
A Child's Eye View

In the Hungate area, children spent much of their life outside. There was no television and few could afford to buy toys, so they had to improvise, sometimes in unusual ways as Rene Sheard points out.

Glass marbles found in excavations at the Hungate site

When I was a kid, I was always with my dad, and we used to go down to the cellar to relieve the mice from their traps. There was tons of mice there. And of course they were all dead, and I used to put all these dead mice, every morning, into me doll's pram, and if it was a wet day, I used to wrap 'em up in Wright's polony skin, and they were me babies. And the next day I used to get some new 'uns and chucked 'em out.

Andy Waudby found out how to make the best kind of weapons.

At the bottom of Coppergate you had Hooks, fishing tackle, guns, you could buy a catapult there if you wanted one. Mind you, we used to make 'em. Used to get elastic off lasses, off their drawers, you can't beat a good home-made one.

Children did not often play games at home, but congregated in the streets, like Lavinia Kay and her friends.

The girls just played around the streets, whatever season. If it was skipping time we all used to skip. You had a long length of rope, we got two girls, one at each end and we'd all take it in turns to wind. Or if you were lucky you got your own. Played whip and top, any old bicycle wheel we could get hold of and we used to 'bool' that up and down the streets with a stick.

Andy Waudby with wooden toy marble rack, 1995

Wally Holmes also enjoyed these street games, though the boys tended to be rather more adventurous.

We used to have what we called 'winder smashers'. It was like a top with a long stem, like a mushroom. When you whipped a thing round there, that really went and many a time your string wrapped round it and it didn't spin your top, it picked it up and slung it, and you heard somebody's winder go. You was off.

Sometimes they ventured a little further afield, like Mrs Kay.

One of our playgrounds was the Bar Walls, just on St Maurice's Road. On Foss Islands, where the iron bridge is that goes over the Foss, there was a canal there, a concrete outcome and there was warm water coming out of there, and we all went paddling, till the policeman caught us. He used to give us a good clip. And we also used to go on Navigation Road, before those flats were built. We used to take a little picnic of bread and jam and bottles of water.

We used to play in Whip-ma-whop-ma-gate, there used to be an iron bar across, right in the corner and we played there for hours, swivelling round this iron bar.

Children at the corner of Dundas St in the early 1930s

Andy Waudby played in the water at Foss Islands, until he had a nasty experience.

The coppers used to chase us there. We used to run like hell over this asphalt. I don't know why we didn't cut our feet. The last time I went swimming in there, there were two or three of us, and there was a bag floating about in the water, and it had got jammed up near the power station, because at the side they had some square thing, a wooden platform on concrete. I think it was where the intake pipes were for the water for generating. These blokes picked this bag out and they split it open and there was a dead pig in, and it was all green and it was a fortnight after, all my face broke out and I had an awful face for a few weeks. I never went swimming there again. That was my last experience of swimming in the Foss.

Samuel Thompson also knew the place.

They used to gamble on Pound Garth, tossing tuppence and they'd get raided by the police. And they'd jump in the Foss and swim down t'Foss, and get out of it down there. It wasn't very deep. There was a little bridge near the cooling tower and we used to swim there. There were all reeds. We used to say, "Are you going bare golly?"

John Waite also liked swimming.

We swam in the Foss regular. And then we used to dive off Layerthorpe Bridge and Walker's coalyard. And the barges used to come along there. We'd go down where the discharge would come and used it as a waterfall slide, it was quite warm.

There was a keen interest in sport, and Reg Deighton and his friends played football in Spen Lane.

Ball used to go over the top cos we used to climb over the big boards to go in. There was a slope and the lads used to play king of the slope, and we'd to get up there and you had to pull everybody down. Of course we'd wear galoshes or plimsolls as they're called now. Jean Bell was the prettiest girl in the street, she lived in Aldwark actually, and she knocked me feet from under me. Didn't try to push, just knocked me feet and that was it, I was knocked off. And I fell down and just punched her one, straight in the nose. And it bled all over. Of course she went home and told her mother, her mother told the school, and the next morning at assembly, the headmaster called me out and gave me three on each hand. I couldn't cry but I was really humiliated. And I've never struck a woman since!

Many children did not have a football. Andy Waudby

Went to the slaughterhouse in Hungate and asked for a pig's bladder. We blew it up and played football. We couldn't afford a rugby ball so we made a parcel of old newspapers and used that.

James Cave

Played on St George's Field, at cricket and football. We must have worn the grass away. Used the trunk of a tree for wickets, used to mark it with a chalk. Used to be at St George's Baths, we knocked a ball right through t'window.

Andy Waudby certainly found plenty of things to keep him amused.

Did you know there was once a lion escaped down Lady Peckitt's Yard? Years ago they had a circus in Parliament Street where the market was and one of the lions escaped and it ran a-ruddy-mok there. And that's where they collared it, in Lady Peckitt's Yard.

When I was a lad there was Black Harry and his 'gunboat', the River King. That's where I learned to scull, on one of t'cocky boats of the barges. We built a canoe, in the house. It was too big, we couldn't get it through the door, so we had to take it to pieces again. Eventually we got it down to Leeman Road, this kid George and me started paddling up river, bloody thing sank.

George Squire too, found other means of entertainment.

I saw a wake in Stonebow passage. Finnegan Brothers took me down and the coffin was propped up down there. The corpse had a hat and brown suit and big boots, and the women were drinking gin out of mugs.

Children in Garden Place in Hungate.

Dorothy Cook and her friends had more gentle pursuits.

*We played with marbles and cigarette cards. We'd pretend to make
scent with rose petals and water in a bottle and shake it up.*

But some girls were mischievous, like Irene Thompson.

*We'd gone into t'churchyard, playing. And they shouted, "Hey up,
there's vicar coming". I was a bit chubbier than the others, they all fell
over the railings and my elastic of my knicker legs caught on it and
pulled me back, and spike stuck right through my leg. They had to lift
me off and take me to hospital. And I had two stitches but then I got a
good hiding on top, for being in there.*

Years later, in the early 1950s, when much of Hungate had been
demolished, Valerie Law would play on the open ground.

*When it was light nights we used to go on our bikes onto Hungate,
which was derelict, with hills, soil, all rubble, shrubs and trees. It was
BMX type thing but we had ordinary bikes and we'd go crashing up
and down these hills and we'd always be getting punctures.*

John Waite recalls getting his first bike.

*The best bicycle shop was Tang Hall tip. We used to go down there
and get a wheel one week, a frame another, we'd paint 'em and make
our own bicycles up. On Saturday we'd go out to Stockton on Forest
collecting rhododendrons, or go brambling.*

Sometimes entertainers would liven up the streets. Nell Fearn
remembers several of them.

*You got an old chap and he used to sing, "O ta-rat-a-ta". Then there
was Burlington Bertie, he used to stroll down with his top hat and his*

coats and do the lot. And then this old man come with his concertina and he used to play it and all the time, he used to go 'huh, huh, huh', you could never hear what he was playing, because he was huhuhing all the time.

When you used to come out you'd say, "Where are we going to stand outside tonight? Where do you think t'best fight will be?" You used to think you were lovely when you were 14 or 15 in those days. We'd go round and get talking to boys and they'd say, "Where do you live?" And we never used to tell them we lived in Hungate or they would say, "That's where they play tiggy with hammers". But it was a great atmosphere.

Occasionally there would be other special forms of entertainment, like the fair on Haymarket, though this was not without its dangers as Rene Sheard found out.

The cocks and horses went right round outside our house. My mother had a fit once. I was outside on these swings and horses, and somebody went in to me mam, "Oh Mrs Wright, there's a man taken your Rene down the yard". Course she was up in arms and me dad was right there and this man was a married man, he lived in Orchard Street. He had eight or nine children of his own, and he'd picked a bairn up. My dad got him though, he was caught running away.

For some children, there was the summer outing to look forward to, and Mrs Kay was lucky enough to go.

They came round and they got the names of poor children. So we had our name down, and on the day of the trip we had to go to the cattle market. And that was round where the Barbican is now, and there was double decker buses. I don't know who organised it. I suppose maybe some charity or something. We had to go in lines of two, and to keep us all in order we were all fed into the cattle pens. It was just like a snake

going round. And as you got on the bus, you were given a brown bag
with an apple and an orange, and a sandwich and a penny. And we
went to Filey, it was the highlight of the year.

Wally Holmes remembers such trips.

The favourite place was Hunmanby Gap. And there we had our dinner.
And it was allus Wright's sausage rolls, and Wright's pork pies, which
was given by Wright's freely to poor children of York.

Sunday Schools also organised outings and Louisa Aldrich went
along.

Reverend Smith was the vicar of St Saviour's Church. He organised
a party of us to go by bus to Filey for the day. We got a penny and
then we got ice-cream when we got there. We had a right good time on
t'beach.

For Alice Butterworth it was the country rather than the sea.

We used to go to the Band of Hope and Sunday School down a passage
there, that was our Hungate Mission. If we went out on a Sunday we'd
generally go to Clifton Ings, round Homestead, we never got no farther.
And the Sunday School trip on horse and carts to Stockton Hall.

Samuel Thompson recalls,

If you went on t'Sunday School outing they'd take you on a horse
and cart. They'd wash it down, put a couple of sacks on and go as far
as Strensall Common. Give you a bag of buns and I had my catapult.
Good day out. It was brilliant for us cos we had nothing at all.

George Squire knew one family who had 18 children.

It was the first time they'd seen sausage and eggs, when the missionaries gave them breakfast. There was a Poor Boys' trip to Scarborough and the Salvation Army had parties. There was no fighting because all everyone did was eat.

May Greenley remembers other trips.

Once a year the coalman would take so many kids for a ride in the country for a 'holiday' and picked out a few. They put newspaper down to sit on. I went only once. Used to go to Homestead though on a Sunday afternoon and practise the Maypole. I got made May Queen at Homestead. Had long hair to my waist and my mother washed and frizzed it.

Valerie Law and her sister also enjoyed days away.

As we got older, we went to the youth club at Centenary Chapel. When we were younger we went there for Sunday School on Sunday afternoons and on trips. My mum couldn't go on trips because of the shop, so other people had to look after me and my sister. We had to go dressed alike so if one of us got lost, they knew what to look for.

Others were happy enough to take a trip across York, like Lily Hall.

We used to go on the tram to Knavesmire, and there was a band there. We made daisy chains and wore white shoes and socks and we were all right until we walked into cow dirt.

Andy Waudby got taken on trips, but for him it wasn't much fun.

I might as well have stopped at home, because we'd go to a pub, soon as you got to Scarborough. We'd go for the day and I used to stand outside while my dad went in the pub, and I'd wait for him and he'd give me an ice cream cornet and after an hour or so he'd come out. We used to go on the beach for ten minutes and sit on t'sand. We'd go and get fish and chips then back to the pub and move on to the next pub.

He had a better time staying in York.

During the summer holidays we would take the potato sacks and make tents with sacks and brush shafts on York racecourse, and play cowboys and Indians.

An old soldier befriended him and took him fishing.

We couldn't afford a rod so he taught me to make one and make a float out of birds' feathers. The man brought broken biscuits and peanuts for us both and we spent hours fishing. He taught me to live by a saying, which later helped me to get through and save my life in Burma. It was, "Never let it be said that your mother bred a quitter".

Sometimes the children's pursuits were inadvertently linked to politics, as Andy Waudby describes.

There was the time we used to sit and watch the Blackshirts and wait for them to start fighting. And when they started fighting on the floor, the money used to come out of their pockets. We used to sit there and just watch them. Then the meat wagon came, the Black Maria from the police. After they'd scattered, we'd go and look for the money that had spilt.

John Waite also recalls

There were a couple named Brown who taught ballroom dancing. They had a son and daughter who became very active in the Blackshirt movement at the time. And they used to preach at the bottom of Coppergate and Ousegate where the Salvation Army used to play on a Saturday afternoon. Of course all the young fellas who didn't like the

Blackshirts or who wanted an argument used to get round there and harass them as they were preaching away. In the end they'd have a big fight and the police used to arrest one or two. Sometimes the police used to just let 'em fight it out and stand on the outside and pick 'em up as they dropped down. The Hungate area would all be strong Labour but they had a strong loyalty towards their country and the Crown at the time. And although they didn't care for the Conservatives because of the poverty, they were still not into radical movements. Of those who were born in Hungate and moved on, they could have serviced two or three battleships, the amount that went into the navy alone.

Hungate residents celebrate York Adult Schools Jubilee, 1907. Corner of Hungate and Lime Street.

Pound Garth

One of the few places which was recognised as a children's playground was Pound Garth, a large open space at the bottom of Palmer Lane. It was known colloquially as Pond or Pong Garth. Maps from the early part of the century marked a proposed bowling green on part of Pound Garth, but this never happened. Wally Holmes considered it very important.

Pound Garth was a regular meeting for all Hungate. They was all there playing this and playing that, but the big main thing was tiggy exxy. I should imagine the exxy bit is getting rid of the ball. When you'd been tug, the ball must exit, get rid of it. It was rugby in a way, what they call, union men, touch rugby. Soon as you touch, pass. Well they were on there and they used to come until there'd be maybe 20 a side in t'finish. Especially when the gamblers were playing as well. Pitch and toss club, they had lookouts planted. As soon as the flat feet were coming, they all knew then, look out at signal, to join playing tiggy exxy. And then when police went away, back they went again and carried on with their pitch and toss.

Reg Deighton played on Pound Garth.

Bedern School used to use it as their playing field and we used to have our annual gala when we had races. But mainly we used to go down there on a summer's night and play cricket with a hard ball, and stumps knocked in. We would play tiggy exxy, but instead of playing with a rugby ball, we used to roll brown paper up tight, fasten it with string until it was about ten inches long and four inches circumference, and we used that. There was some good players come out of there, for York Rugby League. Jacky Linfoot, he played for Great Britain, in the first amateur rugby league side that went to Australia. There used to be some really rough games played there. My brother was the captain and they won the cup, [for rugby], and I was a little lad and I was sat on his

51

shoulders, holding the cup on his head, and we went round Layerthorpe and Hungate, and everywhere, challenging them that we'd won the cup.

Lily Hall also remembers it.

We called it Hungate Park. If we'd any games on from school, rounders or anything, we used to go there. We had swings and seesaw and sand, spend many an hour down there. In them days, little simple things you enjoyed. I had some friends that had a greengrocer's shop and we'd sit on the pavement playing jacks. Four little square jacks and you'd a ball. And you put the four jacks down and you'd bounce the ball and you'd pick one up until you got four and then in the finish you had to throw the ball up and catch that and get all four and if you did that, you won. Shuttlecocks and battledore on Shrove Tuesday, and lads had whips and tops, and also played hopscotch with a shiny piece of stone. If you got a crate of oranges from the shop and they were fastened up with band and it was plaited, we used to use that for skipping rope.

Jack or 'alley gob' found in Hungate excavation

But part of Pound Garth was private property, owned by Mr (Daddy) Dowson as Reg Deighton recalls.

He had all sorts in there, he used to have a few hens and a pig. If you went in there you went at the risk of being chased by a dog or being hit by him with a stick. And of course if you went home you couldn't say to your dad, "Daddy Dowson hit me with a stick", cos all you got was, "You shouldn't have been in his place".

The private area did not stop the children going in, as Nell Fearn explains.

It was a proper park. We used to go picnicking there. It had cinders underneath but there was grass there as well. And railed off. But the boys used to break in, and the girls as well.

Andy Waudby was one of them.

We used to make a kite and fly it there. But Daddy Dowson had this wooden fence, and we used to climb over the top, then we discovered if we got a saw, and sawed some of the railing out, then we could squeeze through that way.

Samuel Thompson remembers,

On one side, they used to have their gang. They'd make a bonfire on the other side and one on Pound Garth, and they'd go raiding and pinch it off one another. Pound Garth was ours. We did have fun, there was mischief but no vandalism. You'd sooner help people.

Lavinia Kay had another incentive.

It was like a little orchard. We used to go raid his trees, some of his apples, and he'd see us and he'd have the police round. If Kipperfeet caught you, you'd get a slap round the ear.

The Local Police

The two policemen who are best remembered were known as Kipperfeet and Galoshagob. They were respected by the children and Reg Deighton explains why.

They'd give you instant punishment. You got a clout round the ear, and if you ran away, they used to carry a cape, and whack, it hurt. And there was a police box in Peasholme Green and if you wanted a policeman and he wasn't there, there was a little box and you could pick the telephone up and speak to Clifford Street. And they put a blue light that used to flash, on top. The policeman'd be walking around or on his bike, and as soon as he saw that, he'd go to the box. They were very secretive, you never got inside the premises, they used to always keep the door shut. But you knew when they was in.

And nearly all the policemen used to play rugby for York. I think there was three or four big policemen down there.

Ted Chittock also recalls one of the policemen.

We called him Galashogob. You didn't mess about with him because in those days a policeman had a leather cape and he had a lion's head on either side of a chain that joined it up. If you was in any trouble, he'd just whip you like that, and you felt that lion's head. But they was the law and that was it, and you respected them for it.

The MP for York became Governor of Bengal or Bombay or somewhere

John Waite, 1937

like that. They used to come round in motor cars and they'd let us ride on the backs of them or the running boards. "Vote, vote, vote for...and you can't vote for a better man". And then the next day when they announced it from the Mansion House steps, who got in, we used to go looking at the cars and the policeman says, "Hoppit". You could do what you liked when you were going round shouting and singing for electioneering, but you look at the car afterwards, they thought you were going to steal it.

Nell Fearn knew that you didn't mess with the law.

I remember one winter's night and it was snowing, been snowing like mad. We was on a slope, down off Haymarket. Used to love to go down the slides. And we were doing the slides and Betteridge came, great big chap, and he made us, "Go on, get away". And he went into this little shop and bought this salt and he started putting it on t'slides. Some of the lads started pelting him with snowballs, knocked his hat off and he went for them. Everybody scarpered. And my brother wasn't quick enough, and he got him. He knocked on our door and me dad answered and he said, "Now then, what's he been doing?" So he told him. So me dad says to him, "Hast thou clipped his ear?" "I haven't touched him, Harry". He says, "Right, there, clip one ear and when I get him inside, I'll clip t'other".

Sam Thompson recalls,

You saw all the policemen cos they were on foot, but you had your own bobby and he knew all your names. And he'd say, "I'll tell your mother of you". Never your father! And you'd get a good hiding there.

John Waite describes two policemen he remembers.

They were rather like Laurel and Hardy, because P.C. Dennis was very thin, very pale looking and P.C. Pratt was a fat, jovial policeman with

real flat feet. He lived up in Heworth. Course we wasn't little angels,
but not like they are today fighting with knives. We were up to all sorts
of mischief, from making slides to knocking at people's doors, to going
round the bar walls and causing mischief, so we used to get caught a
few times. And if they had the heavy cape with the chain round it, and
you got a smack from that, you knew you'd got a smack! But you still
had a healthy respect for them. I remember being on the bar walls one
time and we put pieces of dry wood in the little round towers. There
was four of us, Eric Oates, Johnny Oates, Dickie Sawyer and meself.
P.C. Pratt was walking along, and we'd set fire to 'em all, and you
had bits of smoke coming out, like chimneys. He's walking along, but
being a proper policeman he covered the whole of the path, he just stood
in front of us, "What you been up to?" "Nothing". But the bigger
boys behind us, they turned round and run. He knew we'd been up to
something and he did nothing more than swing his cape and hit meself
and Eric Oates and we both finished up down in the grass moat, just
rolled down there.

Andy was more cynical about the police, believing that they were not
keen on Hungate children.

We were poor, and they were all for the rich, the well off. And the poor
had to suffer. If you were poor, God help you. But if you've money and
influence, you were all right.

So if you get a lad who comes from a well-off family and he was caught
committing something, and you got a lad from the poor part, the poor
lad would get the book thrown at him. You'd get a good hiding for
stealing and to cheek somebody you'd get a good hiding. You'd get a
kick up the backside and a bat over the ear'ole.

Now I've been on top of a tram, with kids going to see the football up at
Fulford. And a lady would get on and they'd stand and let the lady sit
down. These are lads out of Hungate. Scruffy lads with their backsides

hanging out, snotty nosed, angels with dirty faces.

Andy was a good singer, and he and two of his friends managed to get into the church choir and he felt very proud to be a choirboy –

Until people complained about our haircut and they threw us out. I felt sure the Lord didn't mind our haircut but the snobs did.

Not everyone respected the police as Rene Sheard points out.

There was one certain person on Haymarket, she liked a drink. Then she'd quarrel with anybody. The police were always there Saturday nights. She'd go upstairs, and then emptied the water closet on the coppers' heads. "Get out, yer so-and-so's, get away, clear off". She really was a nice person, but when she'd had a few, she'd row with her own shadow.

Feasts and Festivals

There were some special occasions for children during the year, and the most important was Christmas. Alice Butterworth remembers.

We used to get orange and apple, a few nuts and a new penny, a bit of Christmas cake and a bit of cheese wrapped up and that was our Christmas stocking. But we thought as much about them as what they do now, with all these toys and things.

Lavinia Kay enjoyed it too.

They really had Christmas. People had parties and for us children, we'd just hang one of me dad's socks up, and in the toe of the stocking there was always a shiny threepenny bit. And there was an apple and an orange, a brand new hankie which was beautiful, and a bit of tinsel on top. As regards our family, there was three of us, my mum used to say, "One year it's your Christmas, the next year it's her Christmas", and that person got a big toy. But the other two had to make do with the stocking. And the next year it was the other one's turn. But they always managed to get a present everybody else could use so you weren't really left out. If it were a pair of roller skates, everybody used them. Christmas cake time, we all had to freeze to death while the Christmas cake was cooking in the oven. She really had it off to a T, did my mum. She'd build the fire up, get it to a temperature, all by guesswork, and she'd mix the old Christmas pud. We all had a stir and nobody dare move in the house. We was all banned from the kitchen, we were made

Lavinia Kay, 1995, and (right) as Lavinia Lawson with her mother and sisters, Haymarket 1932

*to go into the other room. And nobody dared even open the door in case
it altered the heating of the fire. But sighs of relief when me mother said,
"It's finished", and that was done solely in the fire oven.*

John Waite recalls,

*Salvation Army used to have a Christmas party for people from
Hungate and Navigation, places like that. And we used to go out to
Gillygate to the big hall and they'd have rows of tables and you'd have a
Christmas party there of cakes, buns, an apple and orange, and singing
Christmas carols.*

Louisa Aldrich remembers Bonfire Night in Hungate.

*We used to collect what we could, put it on one great big bonfire, and
have little sparklers. We collected 'em up and shared them, as far as
they would go round. A great big bonfire it was, I don't know whether
it was where Rieveley's had their hay, a bit of spare ground there.
Somewhere about the middle part of Hungate.*

Mrs Kay also had a good time.

*There was always a bonfire on the park, and there was always one
down Garden Place, round through Garden Street, and what went into
a square. They weren't very big ones. Nobody was afraid of fireworks
in those days. You were lucky, you got a dozen, and bangers, and
your parents just give you matches and you let them off. I can't recall
anybody getting burnt by them.*

*Pancake Day, I mean that was really a day was that. Everybody had the
pancakes. And maybe some of the streets would have a party. We did in
our little street. They used to bring their own tables out and set them
down the middle of the street, and all the kids would sit and the mums
would come out with the frying pan with the big pancake in, tipping
them out.*

There were some organised activities too, as Louisa Aldrich points out.

Lads used to go to Scouts and we went to Girl Guides. There was a building at bottom more or less in Spen Lane, and we went back way to that, some sort of big church that faced St Saviourgate.

James Cave went to St Saviour's Church,

Because it was across the road. But I went to Boys' Brigade at Centenary Chapel. I didn't actually join Boys' Brigade, I had a short spell and got a bit cheesed off with the discipline. Used to have a belt and a round pork pie hat. Very popular, more than the Scouts, who had their headquarters in St Saviourgate.

The Boys' Club

Many of the young boys in the area were able to join the Boys' Club which was run by Hungate Mission. The Mission was actually started in 1861 as Salem Mission, in St Saviourgate, although it came out of a Sunday School in Wesley Place which had 600 pupils in 1822. It later moved to Garden Place. In 1880 the Mission began the occasional provision of free breakfasts for poor children. In January and February 1893, there were 4,660 free breakfasts given to children of the area! A Girls' Mission School was formed near Bedern in 1862. Both Missions promoted temperance. The Boys' Club offered a gym, billiard and games room, drama room, woodwork and handicrafts.

George Squire can remember,

The Prince of Wales, who became King Edward, opening the Boys' Club and coming down in a big car.

Mrs Kay also saw the event.

I remember him coming plain as day, as though it was yesterday, and he was stood there and had a black coat on with a black astrakhan collar, and a black astrakhan hat. I remember him cutting the tape. But us girls wasn't allowed to go in because it was a boys' club.

Hungate Boys c.1930

Someone who did go to the club was Ted Chittock.

There used to be a big place what they called the Hungate Adult School. And people, the adults, used to go up and get educated. But they changed this into the York Boys' Club. It started with a Sheffield Wednesday player who was crippled, called Joe Harrison. Now people who backed the club, was Noel Terry from Terry's, Harris who was chairman of Rowntree's in those days, and Lumley-Dodsworth's two daughters from Bishopthorpe. There was prominent people who put money into it, and we had a massive gymnasium upstairs, boxing, everything. We even put plays on. We had a fantastic time. I remember the last one we did, with me brother and I, we was the bad men in the 'Babes in the Wood'.

Now that was the focus of everything in Hungate. I believe you had to be 13 years of age to belong to the club. and it was a very good thing because, although I don't think there was much crime in Hungate, but you tended as children to get into scrapes where the police was brought down. In those days there was nothing like going and complaining to the Chief Constable or anything like that, about the policemen, because your mother would take you aside and give you another bat if you'd done something wrong. It was as bad as that.

The Boys' Club brought up a lot of boxers. One of the main instructors there was a man called Boy Watson. He used to work at Rowntree's and was a good boxer and a gentleman. I remember in those days the men fighting was Joe Routledge and another man called Harry Ainsworth. They was always on the bill of fighting. And invariably Joe won. He was a very, very good boxer. Come the war, Joe went straight in, was captured at Dunkirk, escaped from the prisoner of war camp to Switzerland and got back home again. Joe died a few years ago. He worked at the carriageworks with us, and was the nicest man you could wish to meet.

Chapter 3

Schooldays

There were several schools in the parish in the early 20th century. Some Hungate children attended Bilton Street School in Layerthorpe, others went to Castlegate School, and one or two even ventured further afield to Fishergate. The Blue Coat School in Peasholme Green (now partly occupied by the York Archaeological Trust) was in a category of its own. But the two most popular were the Haughton School in St Saviourgate for people with money, and Bedern School.

Slate pencils found in the Hungate excavations

Haughton School

Haughton School was founded in 1770 by the benefactor William Haughton, a York citizen, who died at Coldbaths Fields in Middlesex three years later, and was brought back to be buried in Minster Yard in 1773.

He invested a considerable sum of money for the education of 20 boys of the parish of St Crux, providing places for boarders and day pupils, and the school was divided into preparatory, junior and senior. There were many governors including the Lord Mayor, the Recorder, the Rector and churchwardens of St Crux, and the overseers of the parish. The School was run by Mr G H Golledge for many years and old pupils were invited to join the Old Haughtonian's Association. The school started out in St Crux Schoolroom, but by 1901 was housed at 31 St

Saviourgate, a three-storey building with five bays at the front, built in 1735, and extended in 1739 (a rainwater head above marks this date). It later became a mixed school and Rene Sheard, whose father ran the Woolpack Inn on Peasholme Green, attended. Her education was paid for by rather unconventional means.

We had a good schoolmaster, Mr Golledge. My education was paid for by my schoolmaster's scotch whisky and Guinness. He used to come in at dinnertime when the school was empty, stand against the bar. His usual order was a double whisky and a bottle of Guinness, and that was it. And my education was paid through that bill, no cash passed over. All the business people that had children, nearly all went to Haughton School because it was so near. We had a good education, a marvellous education.

Jack Birch, who lived next door to the school, remembers the whole family being taken there during the course of an air-raid in the First World War.

In June 1916 when I was just over five years old, I remember being woken in the night and being taken downstairs. And we were taken, the whole family, into the next door property which was Haughton School, run by Dr Golledge. We finished up in the basement. Incidentally there were no sirens. The indication of an air-raid was that the electricity was turned very low, then came up again, then it was turned out. It was possible to do this because the power station in Foss Islands Road generated direct current. What I remember was that the basement or cellar seemed quite a sizeable place. It's probably in fact very tiny. But Dr Golledge, very hospitable gentleman, produced baked potatoes in the middle of the night and that really stuck in my mind.

Valerie Law who lived in the shop opposite in the 1940s, delivered groceries to the school.

T⸬ʰᵉ Haughton¶School

ST. SAVIOURGATE, ———— YORK.

FOUNDED—1770.

Headmaster—G. H. GOLLEDGE, University of Durham.

THE SCHOOL PROVIDES A THOROUGH ENGLISH
AND SECONDARY EDUCATION.   SPORTS.

THERE ARE PREPARATORY, JUNIOR, AND SENIOR
SCHOOLS, FOR WHICH THE FEES ARE RESPECTIVELY
2, 2½, & 3 GUINEAS PER TERM FOR DAY PUPILS.

BOARDERS   -   -   -   FROM 20 GUINEAS PER TERM.

——o——

PARTICULARS FROM THE HEADMASTER.

Haughton School advertisement, York City Yearbook, 1921

It was dark and dingy in there with lots of panels in the hallway. It had a staircase going up and there was a lovely big balcony. Later on, children used to go there to sit for piano exams. A girl who came to see me, said there was a great big skull on top of the stairs. The first exam she sat, she failed, and her mother was convinced it was because of this skull that frightened her.

James Cave recalls a tragic incident during the First World War connected with Haughton School.

I remember Zeppelins coming over, passed over the back of houses in St Saviourgate. There was a couple stood in the doorway, a soldier and his young lady, at the end of St Saviourgate, and the bomb dropped and blew her foot off. And the foot landed through the Haughton School window and our headmaster actually picked it up.

He also remembers,

You started school at four, at least thirty in a class. We started 9 to 12, then 2 to 4. Kids came from villages, a lot from Dunnington, Osbaldwick, Sheriff Hutton. These boarded. Every Friday morning they used to read us one of the Sherlock Holmes stories.

Bedern School

In sharp contrast, most of the local children went to Bedern School, on the corner of Bedern and St Andrewgate, where conditions were not particularly good. Like most schools in the Victorian period, and the early years of the 20th century, discipline was strong and children feared their teachers. Bedern had the added 'delight' of its unpleasant environment, not just being situated in a poor, overcrowded area, but close to the slaughterhouses, whose aroma even invaded the classrooms. Lavinia Kay talks about her time there.

I started school when I was three years old. I'd be about five years old when we started lessons. It was, to my way of thinking, a very nice school. There was only one teacher I didn't like because he used to give us the cane. If you was ever caught whispering, to the front, and whack, the cane on the hand. Near school was a slaughterhouse, and we didn't like the animals being slaughtered. We used to come out from school and they used to be swilling the streets after they'd slaughtered the animals. And that was in St Andrewgate, right opposite Bedern School.

We were taught just the fundamental things. We were taught to read, write, say the three R's, writing and arithmetic. We were taught the basics of learning how to keep house, and sewing. We were taught to swim. But above everything we were taught to keep house. And from that school I went to St Denys School in Piccadilly.

Ted Chittock was another pupil of Bedern.

I remember playing truant with a man for three days off school, and me mother couldn't believe it when she took us to school and she found out we had. And the headmaster said, "I'm going to give them a severe caning". And when we got home me mother asked us if he had, and I says, "Yes", and me mother gave us a good hiding as well.

The first electric lighting on the scene was when we went to Castlegate School and they used to sell scent cards, impregnated with scent, penny a piece to buy electricity for the school.

We then went to St Denys School, that was the senior school. They wasn't interested in academic studies at all. Your mind was tuned more or less to sport. I used to swim for the school, play cricket, soccer and rugby, and we used to go up to a place called Fenby Fields at Fulford, which was back of Lord and Lady Hatcherley's, right near St Oswald's Church.

May Greenley went to Bedern School when young,

> *But when I was about eight, I left for Castlegate. Mother used to go into Bedern School and get me to go to the shops. "Hurry up our May, and go to Wright's for a pork pie". I took a jug and got a drop of gravy. But it was different at Castlegate. I got the cane once as I put a worm in teacher's inkpot and the teacher's daughter sat next to me and told. But I won a prize for a Brooke Bond writing competition for schools in York.*

> *At Bedern it was there we signed the Pledge, aged eight or nine.* [This was against alcohol. The Band of Hope in particular promoted strict temperance]. *And anyone who signed the pledge got a free holiday. I went on a stagecoach to a woman called Mrs Bunney near Brandsby for a week. It was awful. I'd rather have been at home. And I've kept it* [the Pledge]. *Never drink now except a sip at weddings.*

Castlegate School

Mrs Cook went to Castlegate.

> *If you got the cane you never went home and told anyone. You might have got another. Teacher's word was law, and your parents' was too. The teachers were old, had silvery hair. I remember reciting times table.*

Samuel Thompson also went there.

> *Between Piccadilly and Fossgate is Merchantgate. Some steps went down and that was the playground. They tell me there is a tree planted there from the old scholars of Castlegate School. I went from there to Bedern School, then I went to the Model School, used to have to go to school on Saturday morning and have Wednesday afternoon off, the only school in York that did that. We was segregated. They had an A side and a B side, the good ones was on the A side.*

*Above: Dorothy Cook, 1995,
and (right) Dorothy Barker,
Castlegate School, 1930*

The Model School was the Model Elementary School for Boys on Lord Mayor's Walk, attached to St John's Teacher Training College (now York St John University).

Louisa Aldrich was another pupil of Castlegate.

When I went there, there was infants and they were mixed, but as you got older and you went upstairs, they were all girls, but I think that came to be mixed. We used to have a little garden and Craven's sweet

69

shop, factory was there, at side of it. We had a headmistress lived facing the church, a Miss Sylvester. She was strict. But there wasn't a lot of caning went on, because they were that strict with you, you had to do as you were told.

George Squire enjoyed his time there.

Teachers were marvellous. Miss Sylvester was headmistress. Then I went to the Model School, they were too handy with the cane. If your clothes weren't up to their standard, you got the stick.

I went to Park Grove. Everybody in the class had to read, had to do joined up writing. I once got the stick because I didn't like Wordsworth. I objected to reading about daffodils.

Gardening at Castlegate School, 1913

Jack Birch actually walked out of the city centre to get to school.

I went to the primary at Fishergate, and we used to play in the yards, carefully segregated because the boys were in the right hand yard and the girls in the left hand yard, behind the school. And I can remember how all the lads used to play with cigarette cards, accumulating vast quantities of these, and sometimes using them as barter. They might even barter a pack of cigarette cards for tuppence or threepence, which could then be spent on sweets. But I do remember the time when mother had given me an apple which I had in the playground and I'd just finished eating this when one of the lads came up and said, "Give us your core!" Would I give him what was left at the centre of the apple? Which I did. I remember the teacher coming in to the playground and calling all the lads up to listen to some announcement which was on November 11th to announce the war was over. I don't think that any of us really had an inkling what a tremendous occasion it was. But one of the staff, a young lady, just broke down in tears and rushed back into the school and we knew that it was serious. She probably had lost her fiancé in the fighting.

Blue Coat School

A completely different establishment was the Blue Coat School, which was founded in 1705 for 40 poor boys to be 'lodged, clothed, fed and taught'. The same year, the Grey Coat School opened in Marygate for 20 poor girls. By 1818 the boys' school had increased their numbers to 52. Boys were bound apprentices under the direction of the Committee to learn husbandry, manufacturing or trade, some even being prepared for the Royal Navy, And if they were not successful in these areas, there was still the possibility of being put out to service in respectable families. Girls were placed in household service under the regulations of the Ladies' Committee. Both schools continued right up until 1946 when they became orphanages. Many York citizens were educated at the Blue Coat School including at least two Lord Mayors and Rhodes

Ernest Webster, 1995

Brown, founder of W P Brown's department store. When old boy W H Thompson was sworn in as Mayor in November 1943, the boys of the school formed a guard of honour.

A 1907 map of the area shows the school had a wash-house, bathroom, coalhouse, committee room, dining room, kitchen, playroom and masters' room. Ernest Webster was a pupil at the Blue Coat.

We had school in morning and afternoon, just as I imagine the schools in York. But it was separated from them altogether. It was a school by itself. Very strict. You had to do as you were told. For a start off there was particular times for everything you had to do, like getting up in a morning. You had your own school to clean between you. The boys did their own dormitories out, swept and cleaned once a week. You weren't allowed out at all. Only with a teacher, or there was the eldest boy took charge.

It was a big school, a big playing area. It was quite a nice place though I can't say that I liked it very much. You see the discipline was too much. Elmpark Way used to be the Blue Coat School cricket ground. Now in the corner used to be Amos's cottage and he was an ex-Blue Coat boy. I remember the R101. We all went outside in the school yard to see it. It blotted out the whole sky. Somewhere near dinnertime it came over. It was a sight to see.

Five o'clock was the getting up time, but everyone had to be out of the bedrooms by six, and all the beds had to be made up and the dormitories left clean before they ever attempted to come out of them. We went to church twice every Sunday, morning and afternoon, to St Michael's.

You'd no fires. Everybody had to go into the day room at seven o'clock, they had to be there, dressed, washed and everything. They'd see you'd cleaned your boots, polished 'em. They were given a good inspection. Yes, there was nobody in that school that went out dirty. I can tell you that now. The meals weren't bad. You were never hungry. When you finished your meal, you'd had sufficient.

Mr Webster's daughter admired the other skills that he had learned at the school, such as cooking and sewing, skills that boys did not usually learn elsewhere, and the sense of independence it brought.

It was a good upbringing. I'll give you an instance. My dad can sew, iron, cook. When I mean sew, I don't mean on a sewing machine. He can actually get the whole thing out. Leatherwork, craftwork, woodwork, metalwork. You name it, they did it. If they wanted anything repairing, they did it themselves. If a chair broke they'd mend it.

But Mr Webster also explains that many boys were unhappy there, even though they probably had more food and better clothes than others in the Hungate area.

I ran away three times. I got a good thrashing when I got back. They caught me somewhere near Doncaster. As a youngster you never think. Get away from t'school as fast as you could. I'm afraid I was the ringleader. I took ten boys with me, but we weren't out long, I can tell you.

The only thing is, if I'd known then what I know now, I'd have been straight to the authorities. My back was absolutely red raw. Oh I'll never forget that thrashing. I'll never forget the fella that did it either. He never came anywhere near me when I was grown up. I never saw him. I would have belted him if I had. I don't know what my back must have been like, stripped down, your shirt off, and hitting me with a cane. I'll never forget it.

You couldn't go to your parents or anything, unlike the kids at Bedern School. They got good thrashings there as well, but they went straight home and either the parents agreed with the teacher and gave 'em another one for being naughty or their dad would be straight up to Bedern School and knock the living daylights out of the teacher. But you couldn't turn to anybody.

Yet despite this dreadful treatment, the strict discipline and the stigma of being known as an orphan, he concedes that the regime did equip boys for the harsh world outside.

It was a tough school was that. You knew you'd been to school. You was really taught, no doubt about that. Because we used to have 'em after tea, well nobody in York schools had lessons after tea. But they found us a job. You had a trade really when you left school. You could go anywhere. In fact a lot of the people in York that had workshops, used to try and get you on their list, for to go and work for them. We did everything you see, everything.

Chapter 4
Industry and the Workplace

The Drawing Office, Adams Hydraulics

Like every other part of York, the parish of St Saviour had its share of men who were out of work. But the relatively small area was a rich source of employment, and the location of several major industries, such as Leetham's Flour Mill, William Bellerby's Saw Mills in Hungate, the Gas Works and the slaughterhouses. Some of these companies owned a lot of property in the area, in particular the Leethams. There were also plenty of smaller employers such as corn and hay merchants, iron founders, scrap merchants, coal merchants, undertakers (often combined with joiners), John Hunt's Brewery (later the Ebor Inn in Aldwark), bakehouses, salt merchants, blacksmith's workshops, leatherworks, stoneyards, wheelwrights, chicory works, and laundries. Some people in the area were also self-employed tradesmen. In 1851 for example, there were 67 shoemakers in the area, along with comb makers, painters, coach trimmers, iron moulders, cork merchants, tailors and confectioners. Adams Hydraulics in Peasholme Green was a manufacturer of sewage disposal plant. It had started out as two separate companies, Kirk's Foundry founded in 1885, and Adams & Company founded 1887. They amalgamated in 1919. Samuel Henry Adams developed the 'Cresset', an airlock pattern sewage distributor and sewage ejector which displaced the sewage lift as one of the company's major products. The company was well known nationally and continued to trade in the area until 1971.

Adams Hydraulics, Peasholme Green

Leetham's Mill

The flour mill in Hungate had been founded by Henry Leetham in 1860. The premises were extended down to the Foss in 1885 and after Castle Mills lock was rebuilt in 1888, the mill was one of the main users of river traffic, situated between the river and Wormald's Cut, with access over a small bridge. There was also a number of warehouses and other buildings in the Hungate area. Henry died in 1896, and a

Leetham's Mill building, 2007

large number came to pay their respects at his funeral. His several sons and their families were able to carry on the business. In 1906 grain silos were constructed and then in 1909 further land was bought from the Corporation. But in 1911 the first strike took place at the mill. In 1916 the newspapers reported that the company had, in their service, the '*Anglia*', (a boat previously chartered to bring Cleopatra's Needle to

England). Leetham's Mill was purchased by Spillers in 1928, closed in 1930 and the chimney demolished in January 1933. There is a large grave for twelve members of the Leetham family in York cemetery, with an ornate monument which has four angels on the corners. After 1937 the mill was used as a store for Rowntree's, but today it has become residential flats. During the mill's time, there were two fires.

Jack Birch remembers:

The firm, [his family firm, Birch's] constructed about 1933, the first part of what was being built for William Dove's in Piccadilly. I remember being on the top floor of that, when we were just topping out, when Leetham's Mill went up in flames. A tremendous conflagration.

I think the silos had been formed with heavy timbers built in a squared shape with corners interlocking. Something started off a fire, which went up these silos, and of course there was an awful lot of wood to burn, and it was a tremendous blaze.

As a young boy, Andy Waudby would watch the workers at the mill.

The windows were high up. Why, I don't know. Perhaps because of the flooding. But then you had the opening to the mill and that's where we used to stand, watch the blokes in trousers and vest. Twelve hour shifts, lifting big bags of flour. And then you had barges come up the river. A lot of people worked there, depending on the mill for a living. But if you'd seen those men, with just their trousers and vest, humping great big bags of flour, it wasn't work, it was bloody slavery.

Mrs Butterworth's father worked at the flour mills.

And we used to go down for our flour. We used to get it cheaper. A lot of Layerthorpe people worked there.

Reg Deighton's father felt he was fortunate to keep a job during the depression years.

He used to be a miller at Leetham's Mill in Hungate and when the mill burnt down, I had five brothers and they was all working and he was offered a job in Southampton, which he surrendered to keep the five jobs in York. Cos in the 1930s it was more important for everybody to be working, than one working and five not. So we stayed in York and my dad got a job at the Gas Company. He used to work for a Mr Blower.

Leetham's had two fires I understand. A small fire, then later on they had a large fire. But not long after, there was an argument about wages. They wanted to give 'em ten shillings a week less than what they was already being paid, and they was organising unions in those days. And they was the first to strike, and what they struck about was Leetham's. It was certainly dangerous work. Mr Chittock's elder brother lost part of his thumb at the mill, and Mrs Thompson's father lost his finger there. But me grandfather had spent much of his life in the place. It had a big chimley. My Granny and Grandad lived in Dundas Street, and when they pulled the chimley down, he was in bed, very ill, at the time. And he got up out of bed and stood at the window and watched them bring the chimley down. He was right upset, he cried his eyes out, cos he'd worked there nearly all the time until it closed down.

The Gas Works

Another major employer was the Gas Company. Gas had first come to York in 1824, after Royal Assent was given the previous year. Initially there were two companies, the York Union Gas Light Company (which had its works on land between Foss Lane and Palmer Lane off Hungate until the beginning of the 20th century), and the York Gas Light Company. These were amalgamated in 1844 and the York Gas Company formed. By 1912 the area of supply extended to seven miles from Ouse

Bridge, covering all the villages in the immediate vicinity. The works were situated on the site now occupied by Sainsbury's on Foss Bank.

Andy Waudby worked there.

After the war I got a job there and I had to give it up. It's big metal boxes and it's in layers. They'd seal these boxes up, and the gas comes in one end and it goes through all this powder, and comes out at the other side. It sort of purified it.

Every now and again, they had to open one of these big boxes up, opened these steel tops off and three or four of us had to go down this ladder into it, and you had a crane which overhung, and we used to shovel this. And you had to break it up because it had gone hard when the gas had gone through. While you were working down there, the gas used to be leaking sometimes so you felt dizzy or sick. You had to get out quick. I went poorly and the doctor told me I had to give it up because of the gas.

Alice Butterworth remembers the works.

It was really interesting. They'd put whatever it was they burned to make the cinders in these big things, and when they was ready for coming out, they used to open it and there was a flame, and there used to be a stream run down and they'd rake 'em out [the cinders] *before they could come to be sold. Then there was Walker's coalyard on Layerthorpe Bridge. We had a pram and used to go to the gas house for sixpennorth of cinders, twice on Friday for two lots of coal and two lots of cinders. And they used to last all week. A lump of coal, a couple of shovels of cinders, you'd a fire going all night in them grates. And we were always warm. You never seemed to feel the draughts in them houses. It was half a crown for your coal and sixpence for your cinders. So for six shilling you'd a fire all week. And now I think it's about six pound a bag or something like that.*

Reg Deighton was one of the many children who queued to get coke from the works.

Every Saturday morning a tanner's worth of coke, and you used to sew two bags together cos you got a bagful. It was no use going with a small bag. You went with the biggest bag you could possibly get. Everybody had a barrer, used to make one. Well we used to have the two wheels and it was good cos when it snowed, you used to pull it, the wheels would lock and it would act like a sledge. You pulled the thing through.

But the smell was rather strong, and seemed to pervade the whole area as Reg Deighton recalls.

It smelt of sulphur. You see coke, you throw cold water on it, it's like oxidey sulphury smell. What happened there, they used to push the coal into the ovens, then push the coke out when they'd got all the gases and what-have-you out. The coke would drop into like a conveyor belt that was running water. As soon as the coke dropped in there, you got that terrible smell come off it. But it was lovely and warm in there on a cold day, used to go in there and stand to get warm while you waited to get your coke. It used to be back of Hungate, the coking yard.

Nell Fearn went there to get coke

Twice a week sometimes in winter. If you had a younger brother or sister, you used to push them there in the barrer while it was empty and stick 'em on top of your cinders coming back. We always had a barrow. Out of an old pram. Get a box, two wheels, Bob's your uncle.

And the men used to fill 'em for us. They were ever so good. You used to take a bag sometimes, hold your bag open and they'd keep putting it in. And you went and asked for so much in measurement and invariably before he closed that bag, he'd dump you some more in.

Mrs Chittock (in centre holding baby) at a street party, Hungate, 1929

For Ted Chittock, memories of the works are much less happy.

I belonged to a family of eight. My father was scalded to death when I was four, at the gas works, something like six months before the Workmen's Compensation Act came in. So as a result of that, my mother never got any compensation for eight children. So she went and she sold the Yorkshire Evening Press, in Parliament Street, from all that time ago in 1926 right up to the start of the Second World War.

For women there were few alternatives. Domestic or factory work were often the only options. When she left school, Louisa Aldrich went to clean at a house in Blossom Street.

It was a big house and I got five shillings a week for that. But you was at it from morning till latish at night. But they were pretty good to me there and I always remember they gave me my dinner, but I had to have it in a room on my own. Couldn't have it with them, weren't allowed that.

And then I went to Armstrong Oilers on Lendal Bridge and worked there. That was four and eleven a week. I got fed up of long hours. It was eight till five or six at night. Worked right through, just breaked to sit down for your dinner and that was it. We made oilers for trains, for the axle boxes. It was very dirty and heavy, often got cut with steel. A long length of steel on a machine; put it in a certain hole to get a bend on the end of it to a certain length. They was all riveted together, and then they were padded with wool and the feeders used to hang down.

Mrs Hall says,

I would have liked to have taken hairdressing up but in them days it was factory work. I left school at Christmas and started at Terry's. We had to go to Layerthorpe Bridge to catch a bus to Bishopthorpe factory. I think it was tuppence. We didn't get much in wages, it was eleven shillings and that was with a Saturday morning as well.

Reg Deighton lived next door to Clancy's rag and bone merchants in St Andrewgate.

Mrs Clancy was a rather large woman who used to sit in the office and pay you for the rags and rabbit skins you'd take in. Jim, her husband, used to do all the hard work, hanging the rabbit skins, and sorting the rags and the iron from the brass and copper. And he used to do all the loading of the wagons. She used to just sit in the office and pay the money. And twice a week one of the jobs I'd do for Mrs Clancy, I used to get a penny, was to go to Davy Hall in Davygate and buy a jug of soup with a dumpling in it, and that used to be their lunch.

Lavinia Kay also remembers Clancy's.

The only time we ever went was when they started pulling the houses down. And us kids what was left, we'd get buckets or any old container, and go round the old rubble and pick up any old piece of iron we could find, nails, anything that Clancy's would take, and we'd get money for it.

Slaughterhouses

Another main source of employment in the area was rather more unpleasant, with even more dreadful smells than the gas works. Reg Deighton describes it.

At the back of the house there used to be Pump Yard, where there was three slaughterhouses, where cattle was slaughtered and taken in York market on a Saturday to be sold.

The worst smells used to come from the slaughterhouses, which was out and about all over the place. Bowman's used to slaughter at the end of Bedern. And then Wright's pork butchers used to slaughter in Aldwark. It used to smell awful, specially when they was boiling the pigs. They used to kill the pigs and then boil 'em to scrape all the bristle off 'em. And it was a smell I never used to like.

After market day they all used to be driven through the streets. There was no carts or anything like that to deliver 'em. Now the worst thing I can remember about that was the back of the Shambles, where Newgate Market is now. That used to be a big corral for the cattle. All the slaughterers in t'Shambles, about five or six, used to slaughter the cattle themselves, using the same slaughterhouse in many cases, but different butchers. And they'd drive the cattle up and into the Shambles into this big compound sort of style, and they'd turn them loose in there. And when they wanted them they'd all be branded with their particular mark. They used to go and catch 'em and pull 'em into the slaughterhouses and kill 'em. And there was no humane killer. It would be the pole-axe. Just pull 'em down and hit 'em with a long spike into the head. That killed them. It wasn't a thing I'd really go and sit and watch. We'd go and sit and watch the cattle coming, but I never really enjoyed watching 'em. I don't think I could have become a butcher meself.

I remember the foul smell was the skin yard just inside Layerthorpe,
where they used to take sheepskins and cure them. Used to put 'em
in lime, in pits. It all used to go into the Foss this stuff, when they'd
finished with it, they'd empty the vats and tanks and what-have-you,
straight into the Foss. And down into the Ouse.

Andy Waudby actually worked in a slaughterhouse when he was
fourteen.

It was real hard work. It was Bowman's butcher's in Goodramgate.
Nowadays they make sausage skins out of plastic, but in those days you
had sausage skins made out of sheep's guts. When they'd killed a sheep,
I used to pull the skin through and then I had to wash it, and it would
be put in a basket. And it used to go to the sausage skin maker. And
there they used to scrape 'em. They'd get the gut, and it used to be a
sausage machine and used to stuff all the meat in and stuff that were in
there, bread and what-have-you.

I had to deliver the meat on a Saturday morning on a big carrier bike.
I used to push this heavy bike all round Heworth with the meat in and
one old lady, every Saturday morning, used to give me my breakfast.
Egg and some bacon, and I used to get a bit of breakfast for nowt.

When Wally Holmes was about nine or ten, he helped out at the
slaughterhouses.

In summertime, holiday time, you'd go to the cattle market on
a Monday. Butchers used to buy their beasts. Well just down
Walmgate on the left hand side, near where the INL club was, was all
slaughterhouses. We used to go round there and help 'em with ropes to
pull bullocks in and they used to have what they called a bell humane
killer. Held it on to the bullock's head and then banged the end of it.

Nell Fearn played near the slaughterhouses.

There was two slaughtering days a week. And we used to go down, and the girls were worse than the boys. We used to sit on the wall and they used to know we were out there, did the slaughterers, and the offal never went into the shops. It used to come out to us. The liver, the kidneys, and the lights as they called them, used to go to the cats. And we used to get all the offal. We'd go with a little bag, and I've seen us sit there on slaughtering day, and we'd take some paper with us to wrap our stuff in. We used to sit on this wall and make boats of paper and there was the guttering where they used to let all this blood and everything run out. And we'd float our paper boats in blood in t'guttering, to see which would go fastest. Red sails in the sunset.

Rene Sheard had a slaughterhouse in the Black Swan yard where she and her family lived.

I can remember now standing watching 'em bleeding the pigs, cos they used to strap 'em down to bleed 'em. Me mam had a pet pig, Bet, which never left the back door.

In 1935 the Council made a new byelaw about slaughterhouses, repealing the previous byelaws of 1890, which required the owners to have licences, and they brought in much tighter restrictions. These included the use of the correct receptacles, which must be cleansed thoroughly and their contents removed every 24 hours. There had to be adequate ventilation and drainage, the whole area should be cleansed within three hours of each slaughter, no pets were allowed on the premises, and, above all, there should be plenty of fresh water available. These simple steps had never before been enforceable.

There were other small employers in the area and Mr Deighton remembers living close to Rymer's undertakers at 35 St Andrewgate.

I can remember running errands for Jack Rymer's mother. She was a big woman with a large chest, and I was a little lad and she used to come about three doors up and I used to look up and I could never see her face. Because I was so small and looked up and everything was uplifted.

Jack Rymer had a big shop at the back. It was a wooden building, used to see all his tools, that he made his coffins. It was a marvellous workshop to go into.

Workers relax in the yard at Bellerby's joiners.

And Rene Sheard recalls

There was a little building which was the Haymarket. Do you know the great big iron weight? That's why they call it the hayweight, where the farmers used to weigh all their hay. I don't remember seeing farmers with loads of hay, but this little railing, there was a man in there of course, checking.

Stan Hall was employed further away.

I went as apprentice blacksmith at Wedgewood's on Holgate Road. It was six shillings a week and I had to be there at 6.30 in the morning to get the fires going, and I left at 5.30 at night. Such a lot of horses about, there was Wickham's and Frank Green's on the Mount. They had hunters. Colonel Kirby's at Poppleton Road and Rutherford's coal people in Rougier Street, great big heavy cart horses. Where Lil [his wife] lived, there was Bellerby's Joiners. They had a big black horse and they said, "When t'lad goes home, let him bring it back". I was like a pea on a drum on top. I put some string round it's bit and got up on it's back and riding it down, got over Ouse Bridge and a tram came by and it nearly had me off. Got to the top of Hungate with me, well there was some devils of kids there and they shouted things and it started galloping down Hungate with me and round the corner to the stable, the chap there. And it hadn't been out o't' stable for a fortnight. No wonder!

And Mr Thompson walked from Hungate to Rowntree's every day.

I worked at Rowntree's for 49 years. They could give you two hours' notice. They could sack you when you was 18, then war came so they kept us on. I was lucky. We got called up for the forces and when we came back, they had to keep your job, and that service counted. After two years they started putting you on the staff, so I'd had five years.

In the late 19th and early 20th century, chicory manufacturing became popular in York. The crop was actually grown outside the city, in Dunnington. One of the first York merchants was Henry Wilberforce who operated in Walmgate. Thomas Smith occupied premises on Lower Orchard Street and Foss Bank.

Reg Deighton remembers,

The other place that used to smell, on the front of Foss Bank there was

Chicory Yard. And they used to get this chicory smell coming out of it, which used to be added to Lyon's Coffee, the liquid coffee that you could buy in those days. Coffee and chicory used to be mixed to make a modern drink, and that used to smell terrible.

Laundries

Something of a contrast to the vile-smelling industries were two laundries, the York Sanitary Steam Laundry (formerly Yorkshire Laundries Ltd), just past the Black Swan on Peasholme Green, and York County Hygienic Laundry, round the corner on Foss Islands. In 1930, there were about a dozen laundries in York.
Mrs Greenley's mother

Was head laundress on Peasholme Green, when young, really good at ironing and crimping. She did doctor's shirts for threepence each to wash and iron. They came round with six at a time.

Andy Waudby's mother worked at the laundry.

She was one of the finest in York for steam, she was very clever at it. The Hygienic was owned by Mr Clark. It employed a good few women and I went there for a while. I was a van lad. Remember Dad's Army? Well you know the old man, Jones's van? The Hygienic had a couple of those.

I used to go with John Stringer to Scarborough, to the big hotels to get laundry. John used to wear breeches and leggings. John and me were coming back from Scarborough, we got to the top of Whitwell Hill, the van went out of control in the frost, and we went round and round like that down Whitwell Hill. And finished up in the middle section. It wasn't half hair-raising.

*Yorkshire Laundries Ltd, Peaseholme Green: advertisement in
York City Yearbook, 1920*

Ted Chittock worked at the York Sanitary Laundry.

I left school in July 1936, went to Rowntree's and invariably, from the very offset, you was on short time. You'd go in the morning, go back to work at the afternoon, card wasn't there, you was on short time. Consequently come Christmas time there was a lot of us sacked. We went from there to what was the York Sanitary Laundry in Peasholme Green. I went to work as a van boy. Me wage was eight and fourpence a week and I worked from eight o'clock in a morning till about nine o'clock at night, and one half day was on a Wednesday, when I finished at four o'clock at night, for me half day. Now eight and fourpence is less than fifty pence in today's money.

Some men were self-employed, and had to be innovative, finding ways to make a living. Rene Sheard's father, Fred Wright, was advised to leave the Woolpack Inn and go into business on his own, in the haulage trade. She tells the story.

He didn't start up in the haulage business till quite late, sort of semi-retired, and went to number one Haymarket. And we lived exactly next door to an old chap, he was a cabbie and he used to do funerals. And I can always remember that the seat that he sat on was all glass underneath it, and little babies' coffins were in that little glass seat underneath.

Me dad used to do a lot of haulage for Birch's, help 'em out when they were busy, with him having wagons. He had sixteen horses at one time, horses and carts, and it was a sight for sore eyes to see them all turn out to go to the Stray for the evening. That was their walk, when the lads had finished their work. Many a time I used to go with them on the horses' backs.

Me dad was a bit of a lad. He used to go to a lot of farmers, and I remember sitting round the farmer's table with all the farm lads, the farmer there with the joint of beef, and he used to be sharing the meat out on the plates, and used to say, "What about bairn, Fred? Does she like a bit of fat with her meat?" I used to go around all the farms, come back loaded with apples and stuff, and we had a horse and trap. We had this special horse called Dick, and it was really a hunting horse. Dad used to go to the country a lot, have one or two too many, fall asleep in the trap and Dick used to bring him home, just tip the trap up, tip Dad out.

```
F.  WRIGHT,
HAULAGE  CONTRACTOR
AND  COAL  MERCHANT.

1,   HAYMARKET,   YORK.
1 to 3 Tons Anywhere.   Estimates Given.   Phone 2688.
```

Fred Wright, Haulage Contractor, Haymarket, 1930

Guy King-Reynolds remembers his father renting out stables to Fred Wright.

There was always the lovely smell of horses. My brother and I used to go and stand at the bottom of the garden as lads and it always had an air of mystery. In the very old days Grandfather Reynolds had horses and his wife used to ride. He himself had a pony and trap for going round and visiting his patients.

George Squire's father

Was in the 8th Hussars in the First World War and by trade he was a saddler. He used to sell fish, get a horse and cart and went round villages, a barrel of herrings to Dunnington, Warthill, Stockton-on-Forest. I could have all the fish I wanted. I've eaten herring six days a week. My mother used to pickle them, 24 in a tray. Then second hand furniture, he could do it up because he was a saddler.

When Andy Waudby was ten, he used a barrow to do errands.

If you knew somebody who worked at railway, they had iron-wheeled carts, and somebody could get firewood or stuff cheap, so you got iron wheels like that. You'd go to Melia's or Meadow Dairies, they would give you a big Danish Bacon box, about four foot, and about three foot wide. Strong thick wood. You had to set off and put wheels on these boxes. A barrer was a thing that could save you money and get you things. Come Saturday, "Do you think you could go to the gasworks and get us some coke?" And she'd gi' us threepence. Up Hungate, you'd see all the little lads wi' their barrers, every Saturday morning. And for an extra tuppence, you'd get a bag on top o' that. Now by that time it were bloody heavy. Now you're talking about us at ten years old. We pulled those barrers all the way back to Hungate. We could make about sixpence on a Saturday morning. Then you'd get somebody as wanted some logs somewhere. So we'd walk right up to top of Layerthorpe for somebody to get a barrowload.

By the time he was fourteen, he had a carrier bike,

Delivering fruit and vegetables. I would cycle until 9.30 at night after starting at 8am. I also did cleaning and scrubbing floors for twelve shillings a week.

After that he worked at a place called Mooney's.

I remember being on a machine cutting steel. I was sat there and the machine going up and down. There was this steel rolling out, and I was whistling away, not saying a word to nobody, happy with the world and I got such a ruddy bat. "Gerron with your work, stop whistling, your mind in't on t'job". I worked on a circular saw at fifteen. And this was teak, heavy teak wood. There was a big saw there and a littler, smaller blade. Used to get these big pieces of teak. I was only 15 years old, don't forget, this great big saw going round, and we used to push this wood through the saw and it used to slice the wood till it was about that thick. Then it went upstairs to some women who were sat at drills and they were like little washers, and these were made for Armstrong Oilers.

I used to cut out these pieces of wood, so these women could make buttons. Now these women, there'd be about six of 'em, and they were on piece work. Now you know a tea-chest, I had to fill one of those boxes wi' slices of wood right to t' top, before I got two shilling. So I had to go like the bloody clappers to fill one before I got two bob.

During the depression, men were laid off and unemployment increased. The Means Test meant that people did not receive any more than the very minimum to keep alive. And when, in winter, there was the opportunity of a few hours' work shovelling snow, the competition was fierce as Andy Waudby explains.

Poor fellers, they used to run like hell, as fast as they could go to Foss Islands to get a job. To earn summat. Don't get the idea the people were lazy. They weren't given the chance to work. There was no work, and they had this Means Test. And if a young lass got a job at Rowntree's, the mother or the father was kicked off the dole straight away. And the daughter's money had to keep 'em.

The Yorkshire Evening Press of 16th January 1933 reported a snowfall of three inches, which was received with joy in some quarters.

"Although to some the outlook was dismal, to the unemployed it was quite a welcome sight. The staff at the Employment Exchange were at the offices in Parliament Street before six o'clock. At this hour there were ten men outside and others soon began to collect. Orders came intermittently up to 8.15. Altogether 207 unemployed men were engaged, and the footpaths and streets were cleared of snow by the afternoon."

Chapter 5

A Wealth of Shops

There were many corner shops in the area, and the community could get most of what it wanted locally, without the need to venture further into the town centre. There were also plenty of tradesmen who came round the streets selling their wares.

Mr Holmes remembers some of these characters.

Mr Squires, the potman, used to come round Hungate hawking his pots with his horse and cart. Then Machin used to come round, selling all odds and sods, off his hand

Shop at the entrance to Bradley's Buildings, Hungate, 1911

cart. Sometimes fish, sometimes brooms, sometimes mushy peas, a right mixture. Machins were a well known Hungate family.

Then there's Mrs Sampson, the ginger pop lady who used to sit at end of Wide Yard in Hungate. She'd sit out there with her case full of ginger beer which we used to buy, then we broke the top off the bottle to get at the glass marble. We'd go playing marbles then with the glass stopper tops.

Mr Moore the milkman had a little shop near the end of Aldwark and he used to come round with his milk there with his pony and cart. The shops were very small and they had Cadbury's Chocolate on the glass, you see the same when you go to the Castle Museum. You could get toffees and lollipops and toffee apples.

Mrs Kay recalls:

Pearson's was our milkman, and he used to come round every day with an urn, one that you could carry. And if you heard him coming, you went to wait at the door with your jug, and he used to ladle half a pint out, or a pint, whichever you needed. No pasteurised, no sterilised, straight from the cow. They used to come round with their little carts and horses, and shout 'Rag and bone', and if you gave 'em anything, kids got a balloon.

Shops in Fossgate

Nell Fearn remembers another familiar name.

There was Kipper Jack. I think he was a mute. He used to trot along and he had this big basket, all spotlessly clean, always a teacloth on it, and he used to have muffins in it.

The corner shops usually had signs on the walls outside, advertising various items, such as Lyon's Tea, Lyon's Cakes, Borwick's Baking Powder, Rinso, Min Cream ('Cleans Better'), Colman's Wash Blue ('for snow white linen'), and Wild Woodbines.

Andy Waudby would go into the corner shop

And ask the old lady if she had any Wild Woodbines. When she said, "Yes", we would say, "Well you want to tame them".

To children, the most important shops were the ones which sold sweets, and Ted Chittock was a regular visitor to Alf Huckle's shop, which displayed the familiar Lyons sign.

On the corner of Haymarket and Haver Lane. When we was children, we used to have a bill at Alf Huckle's shop. We could go in there and say, "Could we have those sweets?", and at the end of the week he was paid.

George Squire was not so lucky. He only remembers that Alf

Clouted kids for looking in the window.

According to Mrs Sheard,

On Haymarket there was a small sweet shop, and this chap used to loan cycles out for sixpence an hour, and I believe his name was Mr Moore. And he also had a little shop in St Saviour's Place near the Woolpack.

Jack Birch also liked his sweets.

I remember there was a very attractive sweetshop that sold gobstoppers. These were large round sugary sweets that took a long time to suck to nothing and therefore the highest price, they were about a penny apiece. Probably made a good profit for the shopkeepers because they were in constant demand.

Nell Fearn would go to Annie Binns' shop on Dundas Street, which sold mostly sweets.

Your eyes would pop when you used to go in.

Of course children often had to do the shopping for their parents and Lavinia Kay would be sent to Wright's butchers.

I remember going for pigs' feet on a Thursday. And she'd send you with a basin and tuppence and you used to come out with red hot pigs' feet with all the gravy dripping. They were beautiful. Now that was a meal for us, two pennorth, and that fed us all, with there being seven of us.

Alice Butterworth also did the shopping.

You went to Comyn's for three pennorth of bacon pieces and a sixpenny shank. You knew who was good to you, you used to stand and wait for them. Used to go to Cross's bacon shop in Fossgate, but Tommy Cross had a butcher's shop in the Shambles.

Then Slater's for your flour and your yeast, can't beat your own baked bread. We used to go to Cross's, take a basin for a pound of black treacle and my mother used to bake all her own bread and we used to have hot treacle in cakes for tea, which was very nice. We'd take a basin to Scott's for their savoury ducks and a jug for gravy. As they came out of the oven they were all soft and then they'd put them in a basin for you, and what was left he used to make into cubes and sell them as penny ducks.

Irene Thompson remembers going out,

To the market looking for damaged goods. It was on until nine o'clock at night. They used to sell them off cheaply cos there was no cold storage. We used to go to t'Shambles on Sunday morning shopping for cheap meat. And fish and chips, tuppence for fish and a pennorth of chips. Wright's butchers at top of Aldwark had 30 or 40 pigs hanging there. We'd go to Wright's on a Monday morning for pigs' feet.

Louisa Aldrich was able to buy a lot for a penny in those days.

Sweets for a week. We got them from Sally Dixon's and there was another shop, we used to call him Greedy Amos. He was greedy as well. At the bottom end of St Saviourgate there was Moore's. That was cakes, teacakes, bread and milk. When the market was on, we'd go round and see if they'd left any orange boxes. We used to take them home for firewood, and see if there was any fruit they didn't want.

Mrs Cecelia Felton (left) and Mrs Irene Thompson, 1995

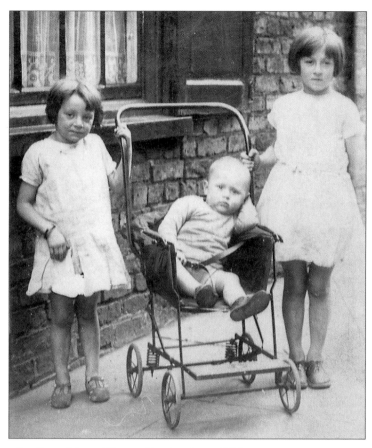

Cecelia and Irene Thorpe, Stonebow Lane, 1934

Mrs Felton would look forward to her older sister Irene (now Mrs Thompson) coming home so that she could go to the shop for biscuits. Irene Thompson explains.

You used to go in with a penny and just ask for a pennyworth of broken biscuits, they'd give you a bag full. And there was machines along on the corner, and cigarette machines as well. I used to go for my auntie's cigs in the machine, Craven A's she used to smoke.

As Cecelia Felton describes,

They were in a little paper. They wasn't sealed up. Just in a little packet with five cigarettes in.

Ted Chittock remembers another shop in Hungate.

Wheatley's, the football player, his mother owned a shop and it was amazing, where they were selling margarine and butter and alongside it was a can of paraffin. They pumped it out for lamps.

In Hungate was Dan's fish and chip shop. You could get one of each for tuppence or something like that. Next door to her there was Mrs Bardy, who made lemonade and toffee apples.

John Waite remembers

Where the Black Swan is now, the right hand half as you go in was sealed off and it was a sweet shop there and bakery. We used to buy a really nice meat pie and a jug full of gravy, and that was called Avery's shop.

Valerie Law lived with her mother and sister in a shop at the corner of St Saviourgate, near Salem Chapel.

Our shop sold sweets, tobacco, groceries, tea and sugar, cough medicine, combs, bandages, a few dolls for presents, drinks, soap, ice-cream. Everything. It was a real good business in 1948 time. My sister and I helped as we got older. There was an old-fashioned till with a drawer, and sliding glass doors on the window. We had to make sure the glass doors were closed so people outside couldn't see us go into the till. Used to have a fire in the fireplace, couldn't have it very hot because of the chocolate. Locals came in and workers from Spen Lane, Birch's, Rymer's, Heppell's joiners of Aldwark.

*Mrs Valerie Law, 1995, with
a photograph of herself as
Valerie Shirbon, aged 10*

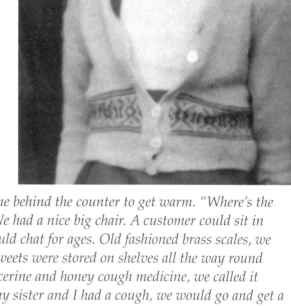

*If it was cold they came behind the counter to get warm. "Where's the
chair?", they'd say. We had a nice big chair. A customer could sit in
it, came to sit and would chat for ages. Old fashioned brass scales, we
used to clean them. Sweets were stored on shelves all the way round
the room. We had glycerine and honey cough medicine, we called it
'icky picky wine'. If my sister and I had a cough, we would go and get a
bottle of that wine.*

*Boys from Rowntree's, the Forestry Commission and other companies
came to Blue Coat School to do continuation classes and one boy
pinched a whole jar of liquorice torpedoes. They used to come at a
quarter past ten as they had a fifteen minute break, and one day she*

noticed there was a whole jar of liquorice torpedoes missing so she rung up. They went down to the classroom to ask them, and they all said, "No". But there was one boy missing, and he'd pinched it and then he didn't know what to do with it, so he ran to Layerthorpe Bridge and threw it in the river. But they made him pay.

The business failed when Carling's supermarket was built where the Halifax is. We bought goods there for Mum to sell in the shop, like six tins of peas as she couldn't afford 48 tins wholesale.

One of the best remembered shops was Billy (Slasher) Calpin's barber shop at the top of St Saviourgate. Wally Holmes recalls people going who wanted

A basin cut, like a Mohican, cut up both sides. Many used to go for a shave as well. There was a hell of a lot down Hungate, the families themselves would drop a basin on and cut round the edges. Then when you was going somewhere special, that was when you go up to t'hairdresser's.

Alice Butterworth also knew Billy.

He was a Walmgate lad was Billy Calpin. But he was there years and years. It was nearly all men. My father used to go there, my husband used to go there, my brother used to go. Billy used to charge 'em threepence for their haircuts.

Nell Fearn was one of the few girls who had her hair cut there.

He was full cousin to me mother, and we never used to pay, he never took any money off us. Everybody went to him. If you wanted your beard trimming, anything, Billy would do it for you. It was a very small place, one room actually. There was these two steps, used to go up and they'd all be sat round this room, and he had a little part off it, where he used to have a sink to wash his hands. There's a programme on television, and it's in America and it just reminds me sometimes of that, where they all sit and talk, nobody goes in to get their hair cut. They used to go to put a bet on. And more or less sit just for company. It must have been a nice atmosphere for them. And how he made his living out of it, I don't know. But he did. And he liked a drop of the hard stuff did Uncle Billy.

Andy Waudby's grandfather had a fish shop at 11-12 Fossgate, with a very ornate frontage which can still be seen.

Waudby's fish shop, now an Italian restaurant, Fossgate, 2007

You've never seen owt like it in your life. It was a big fish shop, all round was game hung up and there was water playing onto this big slab, all the time, and at the side you had poultry. Today if you look up you'll see the German eagle, it's still there, with my Grandad's initials underneath it. And then you had the farmworkers. They would come in a bus on a Saturday. Coppergate most all day long used to be loaded wi' farmers. And they'd stay there biggest part of t'day while their wives were flogging cheese and butter. I always remember the butter all had lovely patterns on, in fact my granny used to love to go there and get eggs.

Many people remember Rieveley's corn merchants, who had a warehouse storing hay and straw near St Saviour's Church. They also owned a pet shop just within Colliergate. Mrs Felton would look in the window.

A window full of little chickens. Little tiny yellow chickens. And there used to be this light in the middle where they used to all cuddle round.

Irene Thompson would also go to the shop for seed for her Granny's bird.

They had loads of birds inside, and parrots and goldfish. There was a big macaw, they used to have it outside on a stand.

Harry Burnett also went into Rieveley's.

When you went in the shop there was sacks of seed. Used to get stuff off floor and go out in streets trying to catch pigeons. You'd ask for sixpennyworth of pigeon pie toffee, and bloke would give you a bat across t'ear.

Pawnbrokers

The other common type of shop in the area, which has disappeared today, was the pawnbroker. There were three local ones, as Wally Holmes remembers.

There were Merriman's, Hardcastle's and Sharpe's. Sharpe's was the nearest of the lot, on the corner of St Saviourgate and Colliergate. A big thing in those days was taking a suit down. Daddy's suit used to go in on Monday morning and then on Friday it'd come back out again.

George Squire was often sent to the pawnbroker when he was a boy.

I took the eiderdown and Witney blankets to Merriman's and got ten shillings, then got told off for being late for school. I redeemed them for eleven shillings later in the week.

Rene Sheard knew of people who tried to pawn clothes unsuccessfully.

Some of the stuff they refused to take in, because people used to take things as husbands took them off, vests and things. "Take it home first and wash it, then bring it back down and then I can loan you".

Alice Butterworth's neighbour was a regular customer.

There was a woman who lived in the next yard to us. She used to take washing in and she used to wash it and pawn it, and she'd get it out again for people to come for it, and then she'd get paid. But me mam never pawned because we'd nothing to pawn. We were always tidy and we'd all be a little bit different for a Sunday from what we used to go to school in.

Shopping in Fossgate, 1905

Chapter 6
Leisure Time

Apart from the pubs and children's playgrounds, there was little in the way of entertainment, and no money for expensive pleasures. But in spite of this, people managed to find ways to enjoy themselves. There was sport, of course. The Woolpack had its own rugby team and there was the boxing practised at the Hungate Boys' Club. Those who could afford it could go to the cinema, and forget their worries by escaping into the latest dreams on offer from Hollywood. There were also important links between this area and the theatre, though for some it was not so much leisure as a means of making a living.

There were other less common pursuits taking place in the Hungate community, such as linnet singing and aircraft building.

Linnet singing

Linnet singing was a favourite pastime in this area in the late 19th and early 20th century. The York Gazette and Herald printed many articles relating to the York Linnet Singing Society and its competitions. Contests were often held at the Black Swan or the Woolpack, both on Peasholme Green. Occasionally meetings also took place at the Slip Inn on Carmelite Street (Easter 1880), the Bricklayer's Arms, Palmer Lane (from 1880 until 1915), the Wheatsheaf and the Haymarket Inn (in 1887).

Reg Deighton's father was a competition judge and he remembers these occasions vividly.

They used to have it in the Wheatsheaf pub. And each man had his own linnet, a cock linnet of course. They used to bring 'em into the pub and put a board in between the two linnets. My dad would whistle to start 'em off. The birds used to start answering each other over the board because they couldn't see. My dad used to judge which was the best bird, which had the largest sort of vocabulary of whistling, because he could whistle like a linnet. This used to happen about every other month, and specially round springtime when the birds used to whistle best and he used to come home drunk. There used to be a row every Sunday he come home drunk, so in our house my mother used to hate linnet whistling. It used to be a common thing for people to have a canary or linnet, a wild linnet, they used to catch them themselves.

Where they used to catch them mostly was down St Nicholas Park, at the back of Layerthorpe, towards Rawdon Avenue. There used to be something the linnets liked on there, and of course the lads'd go and catch 'em with birdlime and nets. It was legal in those days to do it, but you can't do it now.

And they used to have little boxes, put 'em outside and linnets used to whistle to each other. Johnny Smith would have a good bird, so his neighbour would hang his bird near it, so that when it started whistling the younger bird would learn it all. They used to poach the whistlings of each other's birds. So when it was time to start the competition, they used to keep the birds in so the others didn't learn off them. There were stories of Cockneys that used to fetch bullfinches up from London, but they used to burn their eyes out to make them whistle more. I've never actually witnessed that. But everybody had linnets or a canary, used to be fantastic.

The Yorkshire Evening Press described a visit to a contest in April 1908, stressing the fact that singing was not the same thing as twittering. The judges had to be able to recognise the difference.

"A bird might spend ten minutes chattering incessantly without gaining a single point. His opponent might sing a dozen notes and score several points. They are judged solely on the quality of the notes they produce, and the number of changes in their song. The judge can unerringly pick out the good from the bad notes, and can recognise without the least difficulty every slight change in the trills. When two birds get fairly started in their rivalry of song, the judge must be smart indeed to note all the subtle changes, most of them quite imperceptible to the layman. Among the changes are 'cobber's reeling', 'scraping', 'bubbling' and 'whinneying', all of which have their separate values in points. These the judge marks down on a sheet of paper as the birds are calling against each other".

The birds (all male) were brought into the room in twos, and initially hidden behind panels. When these were removed, the judges allowed them to see each other for one minute, then gave them nine minutes to show what they could do. The birds would try to outdo their opponents, in a kind of macho display of singing.

Sport

Rugby was popular in the locality, and Wally Holmes was a keen player.

One of the highlights of Hungate was the Woolpack Inn at the side of Peasholme Green, the landlady being Maud Walker, and the rugby team which came from there was renowned round York area. The Leeds Arms entered the interworks once or twice. But the lads drifted back to the Woolpack. That's the sort of character Maud Walker was, a lovable person.

Ted Chittock also spoke highly of the place.

There was a landlady, Mrs Walker, she was a gem of a woman. Her husband died and she was landlady right up to the Second World War. Even in those days, you come home on leave and you went down the

Woolpack for a drink cos that's where you always started from. And they run the local interworks rugby teams from the Woolpack. That was a famous thing because they used to carry off the interworks trophy, year after year.

The Yorkshire Evening Press of January 1933 reported a glorious win by Woolpack Rovers over South Bank team on the Knavesmire. "The Rovers won 19-3 and Deighton converted the final two tries".

Woolpack Inn, now Jorvik Medical Centre, and Blue Coat School (St Anthony's Hall), 2007

A rather less common sport was dog racing, described by Reg Deighton.

Used to go rag racing, with whippets and cross whippets/greyhounds. They used to just have an old iron mangle, used to wind it and they'd have all the cogs so they'd pull a rabbit skin along the road. The dogs would chase 'em but the original rag-racing was where somebody used to hold a rag and shout, hence its name. And they used to race about 150 yards straight, and the dog used to jump up into the winners' arms. Of course it was his dog. That's how they used to finish, the dogs running up to their owners and getting their reward like a piece of raw meat.

Andy Waudby's cousin kept whippets and they took them to race at Bad Bargain Lane.

One man would hold its neck, and the other man shook a rag in front, shouting, "Hi lass". Each dog had a number on a woollen collar. I would wave the rag for the dogs and got paid two and sixpence.

John Waite sometimes watched whippet racing.

Most of the sport with the men on a Sunday morning would be the whippets in Bad Bargain Lane or Malton Road Stray. They'd race them, come back and go into the pubs for a drink at dinnertime while their dinners were getting cooked. And you'd sometimes see the wives running across from the houses to one of the local pubs, mostly Maudie Walker's, with a little jug to get a gill of beer.

Sometimes boys could earn a bit of money if they were willing to amuse adults, as Andy Waudby found out.

Grown-up men got the lads to box each other with bare knuckles for sixpence, or you could get threepence to get on a box and sing.

The Flying Flea

One member of the Waudby family was a mechanic and he had a workshop in a street off Hungate, where he built an aeroplane called the *Flying Flea*. Reg Deighton describes it.

One of Waudby's lads built it and took it up to the Knavesmire. It was painted red. Great thing to see, it all being pulled down, and he took his wings and body separate and attached 'em on Knavesmire. It had a Norton motorbike engine.

And there was a lot after that, a lot of local motor engineers in York starting building them, and the one I remember was a feller whose son run York Taxis. He built one of them and then he walked into the blade of it and he had all his shoulder smashed.

They had proper fuselages, and the cockpit used to come to about four feet off the ground and they used to climb in. They just had one wing, or maybe two wings, but they was just lads who was experimenting. Engineers who could fit an engine to it and made a propeller go round. Then used to put a body onto it, that's all they were really. I never saw them fly. I read in the morning paper that one had flown in Birmingham.

Cinema

In the 1920s and 30s York had many cinemas. The nearest to the Hungate area was the Electric in Fossgate, which is now Macdonald's Furniture Showroom. It had first opened in 1911, and remained open until 1957 (briefly being called the Scala from 1951 until it closed). Louisa Aldrich was a frequent visitor.

They used to call it the Flea Bin, the Flea House. It cost threepence on Saturday afternoon. Used to go and watch Tom Mix, cowboy, in instalments there. My brother used to go Friday nights and I'd go Saturday night and I would ask him what the serial ended like. It always used to be where he [Tom Mix] was going to his death, but when you got back next week they'd sort of moved it back a bit somewhere and he didn't go over the cliff. There used to be a piano playing music as they was going on their horses, or a violin where the sob stuff came on, where the girl was getting attacked by the man.

For Wally Holmes, Saturday afternoon was a time to look forward to.

We used to go round to the Electric Cinema. Now admission there was a jam jar, a nice clean jam jar. We'd go in there, watch the films, enjoy

*ourselves and when coming out started it was all snap, crackle and pop,
walking over peanut shells.*

The jam jars would be taken to Clancy's, according to Alice
Butterworth.

*At the picture theatre in Fossgate, they used to take jam jars and things
like that for payment, they'd then go and cash them in at Clancy's.
We'd take our jam jars back to the shop, ha'penny for a small one and
penny for a big one. And we've taken rags to Clancy's for coppers.*

Andy Waudby was also a regular.

*We called the Electric Theatre, the 'laugh and scratch'. Many a night on
a Friday or Saturday we've gone and stood in Fossgate in front of the
Electric, in the full queue for the fourpennies. We'd go to Sally Dixon's
in Garden Place there, got a ha'pennorth of carrots and sell these carrots.
We used to queue there and Big Stan would say, "Get off t'flags, get over
here". " I'll tell my cousin of you, he'll thump yer".*

*Stan was the commissionaire. He was a bighead, allus pushing us about.
And he had to keep us in the gutter, away from the flags [kerb]. Anyhow,
we'd get in the picture, eat our carrots, never say a word to anybody.
Sometimes one lad would pay to go in and after five minutes he would go
to the toilet and open the window to let all the other lads in.*

*Then some nights, we'd say, "We're going to the stalls [Parliament
Street market]". Under the stalls, start at one end, cos you had a long
line of front stalls, right past Marks and Spencer's. We used to stand
up underneath and get damaged tomatoes, damaged buns, damaged
oranges and apples. But the stallholders never used to say nowt to us.
Some of 'em used to give us just a bit. A lot had sympathy for us. And
it was wonderful, really wonderful.*

The Electric Theatre,
Fossgate (now
Macdonalds Furniture)

Lavinia Kay remembers the treats which were an added extra.

What we used to do when we went to the pictures when we was kids,
was what was called the threepenny rush, Saturday afternoon. If you
were lucky and your mums could afford it, you got threepence. Or if
you couldn't get threepence, they'd let you in for a penny ha'penny.
But you had to sit on the front row for that. And that was a really good
treat was a Saturday afternoon. Sometimes when you got there, they'd
give you an apple, to go in with, not every time but just odd occasions.

I remember the organ, they was silent movies as well as talkies. It was always a two part programme. And it got packed. They used to come from all over York, and everybody had a good time.

Christmas time we got a treat from them, a bag when you went in with an apple, an orange and a pear. But if you were caught making a noise you were thrown out. You had to behave, and quite often there was quite a lot of them thrown out by the scruff of the neck. But we were always good little children!

Samuel Thompson enjoyed music hall at the Empire.

Florrie Ford came there. We could go for fourpence in the gods, right at the top and that used to be our Saturday night out. Get a packet of peanuts and throw 'em over the top at the people down below. Or we used to go down Coney Street, they called it the monkey run.

Andy Waudby also remembers the Victoria Hall in Goodramgate, one of York's first cinemas, which opened in 1908. It closed in 1930.

And the Victoria Palace, Pally, got on fire at one time. That was a bit earlier, well when I was a kid it was closing then.

May Greenley went there on Saturdays.

All the entertainment was Victoria Hall. Penny in the bucket. We were lucky if we went, Grandma used to give us a penny. Silent pictures, I remember who was on, Pearl White.

The rear entrance was actually in Aldwark, and Mrs Aldrich knew of it when it was also briefly called the Scala (1928-1930).

There was a picture house in Aldwark, the Scala, but I don't think a lot remember that one.

Reg Deighton could see the cinema from his house.

*My sisters and I used to have to go to bed early and on a Saturday
night we used to look straight across from our bedroom into the Albany
Hall windows and watch 'em dancing, and of course we used to do
that until we fell asleep. Next to the Albany Hall was the back of the
Scala Cinema. It was empty at the time, but it was still a cinema. The
entrance was in Goodramgate, but all the fire exits came out at the back.*

In later years, some people ventured further afield. Valerie Law
went to the Regal in Piccadilly (which became the ABC in 1961, and
is now Marks & Spencer) with her sister, although it occasionally got
flooded.

*The lady there used to say to my Mum, "Are you sure she's not 12?",
because I was tall. "No, she's not 12". And when I was 12 [the age
for full price], I took her my birthday cards to show her. We went to
ABC Minors on Saturday morning. It was the children's show and if
it was your birthday you went up on the stage and they sang 'Happy
Birthday' and you might get a present.*

Most people couldn't afford to pay for their entertainment, and when
they started courting, the most common practice was to go for walks.
This was not without its hardship as Lily Hall recalls.

*One night we walked all round Heslington and it was freezing and we
stood canoodling in a lane. Once we got lost up Tang Hall Lane, a fog
came down. [And Stan Hall] climbed up a lamp-post to see where we
were.*

Before couples actually started going out together, they would often
meet whilst out walking, and this is what Mrs Hall did.

Stan and Lily Hall, 1995

After church my friend and I would go walking down Coney Street. That's what you did when you were in your teens, looking for boyfriends, up and down, up and down, and then down by the river.

Public Houses

St Saviour's parish in 1900 certainly had a profusion of public houses and there were dozens more down Fossgate and Walmgate. By 1920, the *Square and Compass* in Wesley Place, (1911), the *Duke's Head* in Aldwark, (1903), the *Whale Fishery* on the corner of Haver Lane (so called because the landlord had been a harpooner in the polar seas) which later became the *Cotherstone*, and the *Old Sand Hill* in St Andrewgate had all disappeared. But a number of inns remained. Aldwark still had the *Rose and Crown*, which was in front of the Merchant Taylor's Hall (until 1932), the *Leopard*, and the *Red Lion*. Palmer Lane boasted the *Bricklayer's Arms* until 1937, and the *Garden Gate* stood at the top of Carmelite Street between that street and Garden Place, until 1938. The name was rather more salubrious than the actual property, which was nicknamed the Rat Pit. The *Turk's Head* was still in St Andrewgate until

1928 (replaced today by Turk's Head Court), and the *George Hotel* stood on the corner of Whip-ma-whop-ma-gate (now the Halifax Building Society). The *Wheatsheaf* was situated in Hungate itself until 1938, with a popular beerhouse, the *Sportsman*, there until 1912. There were three pubs on Peasholme Green – the *Woolpack*, which was rebuilt in the 30s and sold in 1975 to an insurance company, the *Leeds Arms* which closed in 1935 but was not demolished until 1966, and of course the *Black Swan*, the only pub which remains.

Rene Sheard was born and brought up in two pubs.

I was born in the Black Swan, 1911. We stayed there for about four years and then we moved across the road to the Woolpack Inn, where quite a lot of the customers from the Black Swan followed my dad. It was sort of one big happy family. They were such friendly people. When the men were leaving work from Leetham's Mill in Hungate, the clatter of the clogs across Haymarket was really noisy. And there was one man, especially at payday, he would come straight to the pub for his beer. My father was very understanding, and he knew that he had a large family, and he couldn't afford to be drinking, so he always used to say to him, "I'll let you have one pint now, go home, take your money to your wife, then come back if she gives you any change".

There was a tiny little bar, it only seated about four people, and then there was this shelf, the counter with the till underneath it. One of the old fashioned tills you pulled down. I can always remember there was coppers and small silver on the shelf near the glasses. One day he caught a chap with a stick with a bit of chewing gum, sticky stuff, dabbing to get the money. We had the old-fashioned pumps for the beer, with a tray and the old mugs underneath. As soon as I realised, I were drinking out the mugs. Mother didn't know where to find me. I was fast asleep, couldn't wake me up. I was kalied [rather drunk].

The inside of the pub was very comfortable. There was a little passage

*you entered, and the men's dominoes on the left hand side, and then
there was the bar in the middle and a little private room, the best room;
and behind that was a massive ballroom, a great big long room, like a
concert room with a stage at the end.*

*There was a yard where the beer used to be delivered, and of course I
was always up there, always noseying. There was this long passage
from the bar up to the cellar. Me mam used to have a lady helping her,
she used to do the washing up there. And dad used to keep his hundred
proof spirits in the big stone jars behind a curtain in the living kitchen,
which looked right onto Haymarket. Now many times this lady would
be fast asleep in a chair. She'd been helping herself to the proofed stuff.*

*The policemen always came in twos to the pub. Always made
theirselves at home in t'kitchen with pints. I was pulling ale at nine or
ten, I liked to be in it.*

Nell Fearn remembers,

*There was a pub at the top of Dundas Street, and the landlady that had
it was daughter to Mr and Mrs Barker, midwife and undertaker.*

*I know it was a pub because they had a big grate that went down into
cellars. Used to lift it up when draymen used to come to put fresh
barrels in. And I looked down there one day and saw a ten shilling note.
And I said to my father, "I've just seen a ten shilling note, I can't reach
it". We got a big piece of string and a safety pin and he stayed there for
ages and ages and he got that ten shilling note out.*

*The Garden Gate was in Brass Rapper Row, [Carmelite Street], just
prior to it all being pulled down. And they used to pull Magnet beer
down in t'cellar. And our entertainment on a Saturday night when
you was older, was these seven or eight pubs and you'd probably go off
somewhere, to the pictures or to the Empire.*

Charabanc outing from the Black Swan

Some people might use the pub as an off-licence, like Mrs Hall's family.

Me Grandad liked a drink and Grandma used to go to the Garden Gate for him. She used to bring him a pint in a jug if he didn't want to go out.

And so did Mrs Thompson's family.

On a Friday night all t'relations came. They used to come about four o'clock, used to be there till maybe midnight. And then they used to go with the jug down to the pub, and get a jug full of beer. And then they'd be all singing and dancing at the end of t'lane.

Her sister Mrs Felton also remembers these occasions.

My granny would make these big meat pies and a big pan of mushy peas, and they used to have pie and peas on a Friday. Real good old days them.

Another lady who lived in a Hungate public house was Violet Taylor.

I was born at Darlington in 1906. My father, John Pritchard, worked on the railway but unfortunately he was taken poorly through

footballing. He got kicked, and his spine was injured. And then he couldn't do his work, so he decided to take a public house. I was six month old at the time, and they took the Leeds Arms on Peasholme Green.

It was a very big place, big and roomy. Mother didn't like it at first, but she had to get used to it, as father gradually got worse and worse with his back being fractured. He had difficulty getting round. Then mother had to look after him for two years and I was eleven when me father died in 1918.

Me father was ever so kind to people in the pub, because it was a very poor neighbourhood. I used to come home from school

Black Swan, 1930s. Back row, left to right– Fred Pritchard, Charlotte Pritchard (mother), Billy Pritchard. Front row – Violet and Doris Pritchard.

dozens and dozens of times, and, "Be sharp, go and see Mrs so and so", a customer, she probably had a baby. And me mother used to pack a basket up, all home made stuff for me to take down to the house. "Now don't stop, but if you can go any errands for her, just do so while you're there". And me father did likewise. We used to have a market gardener that come to the pub, and me father used to buy sacks of potatoes and have them sent to some of the poor people round about.

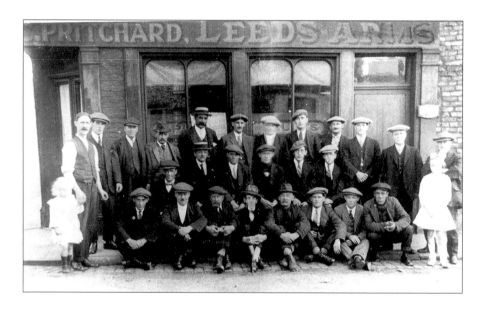

The Leeds Arms Outing, 1919-20

Back row, l–r: *Jack Varley, unknown, unknown, unknown, George Suggett, unknown, Charlie Wilson, George Barker, Mr Galtres, Mr Kay, unknown, unknown,*

Middle row: *Tot Russell, Jimmy Goodways, unknown, unknown, Billy Barker (George's brother), Tom Wilson;*

Front row: *Renee Varley (aged about 3 years), unknown, Jack Wragg, Mr Kitchen, William (Billy) Pritchard, Jack Brown, unknown, unknown, unknown, Doris Pritchard (aged about 8 years).*

By the time I was thirteen years old I was getting used to going into the bar, when there wasn't many people. I was sorry for my mother and I was at the age when I realised that she needed more help. I would love to have been able to stay on at school but I thought to myself I was more good at home helping my mother. We still had a daily person to come, but I worked in the bar when I was thirteen years old, pulling pints, stood on a block of wood.

It was a very rough area. There were such a lot of public houses round us. The Leeds Arms on one corner, the Woolpack on the other corner. Next door but one there was the Black Swan, then the Haymarket Tavern on the other side.

But there was something else that Violet had to do.

There was a hay weighing machine in the Haymarket. And whoever had the Leeds Arms had the key to that place, had to go out and weigh the hay, and keep records of it before it went down to the yard in Hungate to be stored.

Rieveley's, they had a big yard down in Hungate, and a man called Mr.Beck, that lived there, he was the manager. All the raw straw and hay used to come up by the carts, and then it was all stacked, then it used to go out to the farms. And we had to keep the accounts of the weight of it, the date of it, and everything in a book. Me mum used to do it, and when I got a bit older, I used to do it for her.

Pubs were still very much a male domain and 'respectable' women never went into a pub alone. Violet describes the Leeds Arms and explains about another use for the pub.

We used to have to come round the back way. After this little passageway there was the entrance to go into what we called the 'men's kitchen' where the men played dominoes, darts and that kind of thing.

And then there was another little passageway that went off into the top cellar. We had a dining room went off there, run around the back of the men's kitchen. And then you went into a great big walk-in pantry. There was another side passage, but that was always locked up, we never used it, apart from hanging our work clothes in. There was a great long kitchen that went out into the big yard. And we had five stables and they were all let to different work people. One was a coal merchant, another was a fish merchant, there was Pearce's that made mattresses, out of Aldwark, they kept the van in there. Over those stables, there was two great big lofts.

Violet's father was a member of a kind of mason's lodge, the Buffaloes, and was able to offer them the use of one of his rooms.

My father was a member and they used to have meetings in this big room upstairs. It was a great huge room, went all over the lounge, and the bar. And there were six bedrooms as well, up another flight of stairs. And then you went up another six steps onto a landing where this big room went off, and then another door where two more bedrooms went off. Then there was another flight of stairs with another two bedrooms. And all the fireplaces were all black. I had all those to blacklead. All the face of it and the bottom. And I used to make all them spills. In the men's kitchen we had two old fashioned vases, and I had to make all them paper spills, roll 'em, and put 'em in there for t'men. And one particular night, there was four of them playing dominoes, and this chap, he was a customer, he was always joking with me, and he shouted, "Vi, reach me a light will you please, save me getting up". He was one of the men playing dominoes, and I said, "Just a minute while I finish serving". I came back and took one of those spills to light his pipe. And somebody else shouted to me for something, and as I turned round I missed his pipe and he had one of these 'taches that curled up, you know, and I singed all his 'tache at one side. Oh we had some fun. As well as working, there was always some fun attached to it.

One of the public houses also doubled up as a soup kitchen, to alleviate some of the poverty which was being experienced. Ted Chittock remembers it.

The Bricklayer's Arms was a pub during the night but it served as a soup kitchen during the day. That was the main meal of the day for lots of people, because they were out of work and used to go there for probably a penny or tuppence for a bowl of soup. And that fed the family. A very prominent lady ran that, called her Miss Ramsay. She was head of the RSPCA.

Of course drink was a real problem for many people and caused misery for a lot of families. Many people drank to forget their problems though the enjoyment was only short-lived. Yet drinking was a priority with many men and women, as George Squire recalls.

They say soap and water was cheap, but all the money went in booze. The pubs were bouncing with people on a Friday, Saturday night. I used to stand outside. They never had money for food but they always had money for booze, dinner time and night. I used to sit on the wall at the Garden Gate and women used to dance on the tables.

But Jack Birch knew of an alternative.

At that time, gin was relatively cheap, and there were many gin houses, particularly in the Walmgate area. Now the original company called the York Coffee House Company, was created to provide an alternative to drink and they provided a coffee house in Walmgate, with warmed rooms so that men particularly could go and be warm, and drink coffee instead of gin. It became, in fact, quite a successful undertaking and moved from Walmgate and entered into the catering business in the city.

Theatre

The theatre was not really a working class pastime, but as well as the rather more middle class Theatre Royal, York also offered entertainment in the shape of the Empire, where music hall was the order of the day. Many of the artistes appearing at the Empire lodged in the St Saviourgate/Spen Lane area, and caused much interest amongst the residents.

James Cave lived at Rock House, St Saviourgate, opposite St Saviour's Church. He remembers watching from his front room window on a Sunday afternoon and seeing some of these entertainers arrive. Mrs Reynolds even saw Jessie Matthews and Gracie Fields walking down St Saviourgate. When actors were appearing for any length of time, they would put their children into the local school. Rene Sheard met a lot of them at school.

The hours I've spent at the back of the stage at York Empire with these children and their families, because I was always interested in all this dancing business and dressing up.

May Greenley's mother in Spen Lane took lodgers in on Sundays, including one leading lady from the Blue Hens.

She was a right drinker and she was on at night, and she'd been out all afternoon, and she came in and she was well overboard. Me mam and me looked after her and got her coffee and got her sobered up to go to the theatre at night. I remember that cos she was well away.

There were also Russians staying there. They left a walking stick at the back of the door so that it would fall on anyone who came into their room. No animals were allowed but one Sunday a couple arrived carrying a basket. May Greenley describes the incident.

Me mam says to me, "Go upstairs and take them a cup of tea". And when I got up there, there was two monkeys on the bed. She told them to get out.

May Greenley herself loved the theatre. When she was 17, she accompanied a friend who wanted to audition for 'Mother Goose' but instead of the friend, she herself was chosen to be in the chorus. She had to dress as a chicken, and later wear a riding habit.

May Greenley, 1995

I could go for the first house but not for the second. My uncle had to come and collect me at 7.30. I liked it and wanted to keep going but my mam said no, it wasn't right. I got 17 shillings that week.

St Saviourgate had its own actor, Reginald Beckwith, who also wrote plays. He began his career as an amateur with the Everyman Theatre in York Guildhall, then joined Henry Baynton's Shakespearian Company. Several of his plays were broadcast on radio and TV and he went on

May Fearn, later May Greenley, 1928

to appear in many films, mostly light comedies including 'Genevieve', 'The Runaway Bus', 'The Captain's Table' and the thriller 'The 39 Steps', before his career was cut short by his death at Bourne End, Buckinghamshire in 1965 at the age of 56.

John Waite also recalls theatrical lodgers.

My mother took in one or two lodgers. In fact she had one gentleman there for a long time who was slightly related to George Formby, and George Formby's cousin who were both comedians and entertainers at that time.

In Spen Lane there were two sisters, who used to take entertainers in as lodgers from the Empire and the Theatre. Mrs Speck near the old Woolpack used to take them in. I've seen Gracie Fields coming along from there.

Music

Another means of entertainment was music, as James Cave describes.

I've been a musician all my life, as a semi-professional. Used to get half a crown an hour. I started at seven years of age with the violin and carried on for several years and then broke into sport and neglected that [the music]. Then picked it up again. We won the All Yorkshire Dance Competition in 1932. Louis Armstrong appeared on the same night at the Rialto. We were resident band at the Royal Station Hotel for years. We played two nights a week, sometimes three or four, you take it when it comes. Dance bands, the whole of York was keen. I played clarinet, also saxophone and violin. I used to sight read, it was a big advantage. I played with Bert Keech at the De Grey Rooms, the Modernaires, and occasionally the Rialtonians. If anybody got let down, there were two or three of us could fill in, in any position.

We played at a lot of voluntary places including Naburn, Clifton, Bootham, Deighton Grove hospitals. Someone supplied tea and biscuits. We enjoyed it as much, you were free and easy. De Grey Rooms, Assembly Rooms, Albany Hall in Goodramgate, Ebor Hall, Davy Hall, Grand Ballroom, the Rialto. A lot of dancing took place in those years. There were 40 dance bands on one week. Our biggest band was a ten piece. But they couldn't afford to pay too many. I had a motorbike,

*about 18 to 20, AJS and Norton were
absolutely great. I used to go all over.
You could leave your motorbike outside
the house all night and nobody would
touch it. XL petrol was tenpence
halfpenny a gallon.*

Violet Taylor's brother, Billy Pritchard,
became an entertainer in concert parties
during the First World War, and when
he returned to live in the Leeds Arms,
he continued to entertain.

*Billy used to play piano Friday,
Saturday and Sunday nights. Songs of
the day, you know. In our smoke room
where Billy played, you could go round
and there was nearly all young couples
that was courting, and it was a meeting
place for them. They came for a good few years.*

Mrs Pritchard and Billy

*The parties at the Leeds Arms, I think we had about 50 people there.
Me mother had to get special permission so we could have lights on
upstairs. She used to make a big buffet supper, do a great big ham, and
it used to be all got ready and put in the great big pantry that we had.
The main one was always on New Year's Eve, and the pub was open to
eleven o'clock then. We used to go up to the Minster all in a big gang,
all singing, and we used to listen to the bells peal out the new year.
We had two women that came in and we used to get them to lay out
the tables for the buffet. Then we used to have the dancing, and it used
to go on until five o'clock next morning. We'd have 24 dancers on the
floor, we could all get into the Lancers.*

Chapter 7

Health, Poverty and the Community Spirit

Health and the Medical Profession

In the 1920s and 30s, disease was rife, and medical treatment had to be paid for. A lot of people could not afford a doctor, as Andy Waudby recalls.

Fragment of a patent medicine jar found in the Hungate excavation

Disease was right round 'em. These doctors were fighting the disease. You've got the slaughterhouses. You got the ingredients for all the diseases under the sun. But this is life in Hungate. You'll get the old women stood at doorstep and they're all what we call calling [with a short 'a'- means gossiping]. They'll stand there, they've got a flat cap on, they've got arms like ham shanks. Immediately a woman went sick, the woman next door fed the kids and the man. It was fantastic. Oh aye, they'd muck in and help you. There was a lot of this home medicine stuff. Ginger, lemon or summat. You'd dash down to see Mrs Bardy to see if she'd got some ginger.

As soon as a woman went sick, the minute the woman next door would find out, that woman came in to see her before they ever thought of doctors. Because, don't forget, you're having to pay doctors. They had what you call a club, tuppence a week. I take me hat off to these doctors

because they allowed you to pay tuppence or threepence a week. How the doctors lived, well it beats me, because they had to rely on tuppences and threepences to get their money.

Irene Thompson recalls,

There was a lot of illness. Consumption, or TB, but you didn't get these strokes like now. People didn't live so long, they died younger. When you got TB, it's a chesty thing. They used to send 'em to the sanatorium at Fairfields. They used to put you in there and you had to sleep with the windows open. Fresh air was supposed to be the cure. If you was in hospital, somebody'd do your washing and somebody would feed the kiddies.

There was a couple living at the top of Hungate, William and Ellen Barker, who were the resident midwife and undertaker. As Wally Holmes observes,

Mr and Mrs Barker, she brought 'em into the world, he took 'em out again.

Rene Sheard recalls Mrs Barker.

Mrs Barker was a wonderful lady. And she'd a long black coat and midwife bag. My first little house was in Layerthorpe, Radnor Street, and I used to go down to mam's every day, just over the bridge to Haymarket. I'd got down and when I was pretty well away with me pregnancy, mam says, "Rene, you didn't half pull a face when you were going up". "Oh just a twinge or two I have, mam". She says, "Go down to Granny Barker's and tell her". Granny Barker says, "Get your dad to take you straight home and don't come out of the place any more". And she told me what to do with the bed, to get organised. She said I could have had it in the street, that bairn. Anyway it were ten pound born. But I went upstairs and I hadn't been upstairs a couple of minutes and that child was started to be born. If I hadn't gone to Granny Barker's, I wouldn't have had me bed all prepared. And she said, "Plenty of newspapers and brown paper, lass".

When Mrs Barker was called to a person in labour, the beds had to be covered with sheets to prevent the children from seeing what was going on, at the birth of a new baby.

Dorothy Cook was the grand-daughter of the Barkers.

Grandad had funerals. Grandma was midwife. She'd get thirty shillings for delivering the baby and tending for ten days. Grandma used to wear a black alpaca skirt and linen skirt underneath and a flannelette skirt which she'd take off to wrap baby in.

Then there were the school clinics. Nell Fearn remembers them.

York School clinic c. 1918

We used to go there for everything, eyes, teeth, tonsils, manicure, you name it. They'd have taken Uncle Billy's job and cut your hair as well. In fact they used to do, if you went in with dirty hair, they used to take the lot off.

They used to paint your tonsils. Used to have a big long brush and they used to put this yellow stuff on, and it used to tickle, just imagine anyone tickling your tonsils with a brush. I mean kids used to be sick and then they'd bundle you out and he was really mad, used to get really cross with you. And you went to the dentist part to have your teeth done. They used to give you an injection into your gums. I mean now when you go to the dentist, he waits, doesn't he? He sort of rubs your gums around and waits. It was the needle, you was holding onto his hand while he was taking your teeth out. We had it rough.

Wally Holmes sometimes had to go to the 'unction clinic'.

I used to go as a bairn to Castlegate, and when I come to go over Foss Bridge, you can tell how big I was. I used to put me head through, watch the ducks, and everything there, and come back and go over Piccadilly Bridge and down the steps into Castlegate School. Also in Piccadilly there, there was a wooden hut. Now that was the school clinic. They dabbed blue unction on all your sores and everything.

Samuel Thompson recalls,

If you were sick you had to go to the dispensary and you had to get a dispensary note for the doctor to come and see you. It cost you two shillings for a visit. Dispensary notes had to be signed by a vicar, or a policeman, and you used to go to Duncombe Place to the dispensary. You had to go and sit outside in the queue and they'd give you a bottle of black medicine, and the most popular thing was brimstone and treacle!

School clinic used to be in Piccadilly. They used to get a pair of pliers and pop some cotton wool and dip it in iodine, put it in your mouth and paint your tonsils with it. Everybody got that, every time you got laryngitis. And you used to have a nurse come round and look at your hair for nits.

Samuel Thompson, 1995

The local doctors themselves seemed to be interesting characters and there were three who are remembered with affection. Dr Walter Kelly, Dr Reynolds, and Dr Dench, father of the actress Dame Judi Dench.

According to Lavinia Kay, Dr Kelly was a character.

He swore like a trooper. I never really met Dr Kelly until I was about 17 but I'd heard an awful lot about him. He was good with people, he was a down to earth man. In those days you didn't make appointments, you just sat. Anyway all of a sudden, the door opened to one of these rooms and this voice said, "Well if none of you buggers wants to see me, I might as well go home". But this was his manner. I thought he was absolutely great. I never saw another doctor after that but him.

And we were panel patients. Mum paid threepence a week, and it paid for all your medicine. And it paid for you to go into hospital as well. We used to take our threepence into Pavement, there was an upstairs office. We never went to a dispensary because we paid into this scheme.

There was a big flu epidemic. It was before my time. And my granny, she had just had a little boy. There was four sisters and this boy. I think he was a few month old and they had the flu epidemic, and my mum lost her mother, her brother and two sisters all in one week. My mother worked at the Ideal Laundry at the end of Dodsworth Avenue. She was 17. So when they died, my Grandad said, "Right, you have to look after us".

Jack Birch remembers the flu epidemic.

St Saviour's Church at that time was in full use and I remember being in bed in the attic hearing the bells toll for the departed. I convinced myself that I was probably another one of those in a short time, but that never, fortunately, happened. Funeral services were a very elaborate affair, with the carriages drawn by horses, decked out with black plumes, and black trimmings to the carriage. Really quite impressive.

Dorothy Reynolds recalls one evening.

Dr Kelly was going down, he'd forgot the number but there were several lights on, and it was midnight and so very dark, and eventually he called out, "Who the hell wants Kelly?"

Nell Fearn also knew Dr Kelly.

Dr Kelly's vocabulary was noted. I used to work at the Ideal Laundry, and these people that lived in this house up Fetter Lane, we really got to know them. Used to pop in on my way to work to say hello. The old chap there, he was very bad with his chest, and he was an elderly man then, when I was 16, 17, going to work. Dr Kelly was his doctor. I remember him telling us one day that he'd been to see him and he'd leave him this special medicine. He was complaining it hadn't done him any good and he'd been coming over Ouse Bridge and met this friend of his. He was puffing and blowing, so they talked and the friend said to him, "You don't want to be taking any of these medicines. You want to use Vick, don't rub it in, get it by the half-spoonful and put it on the back of your tongue and swaller it". So he did. And when Dr Kelly went to see him, he said, "Well there's been a big improvement here, it must be paying off, this medicine I'm giving you". But he said, "I haven't taken any of your bloody medicine", and he told him he'd been taking this Vick. So Dr Kelly says, "Well go and get another jar and take that, because it's done you more good than this medicine". And that's the type of doctor he was.

Dorothy Reynolds and her son Guy King-Reynolds were exposed to disease because her husband Dr Reynolds had to work amongst it. Guy King-Reynolds recalls this.

We used to catch most of them. Scarlet fever, my father caught that and was sent to the isolation hospital. We all had that. And TB. And evacuate, seal the doors and pump it full of whatever it was, sulphur or something, then we could all move back in. But father had mumps and scarlet fever. I remember father coming back, he knew a family and he said, "I've just been and she's got TB". And they called it in those days, galloping consumption. And I remember a short time afterwards he came back, it must be only days and he said, "There's nothing we can do, she's gone". In no time at all they haemorrhaged and that was it.

Mrs Reynolds remembers

In the old days it was the Guardians, not public assistance like it is now. My husband had a TB case down Kendal's Passage and she had been in Fairfields Sanatorium. And she worked at the Hygienic Laundry and of course with working in the laundry and having TB it came back again. And she said, "Please doctor, don't let me go back". And all the neighbours said, "You mustn't let her go back, we'll look after her". They were wonderful people. Now the Doctor of Health, he was a shocker. He really was horrible and he insisted she go to Fairfield and my husband said, "No, she's not going. She's going to be well looked after, the neighbours say they'll do this and I'll see that they do". "Then in that case we'll stop her voucher". And they had quite a fight. And my husband was on the Health Committee. They had a terrible fight and eventually my husband won. She didn't go and my husband did provide the vouchers, you could not get a thing out of the Guardians in those days.

Everyone admired Dr Reynolds, including May Fearn.

Everybody loved him, he'd come down there to you, no matter what hour of the day or night it was. It didn't matter if you had 200 quid in your purse, or tuppence, you was his patient. He was a marvellous man. No discriminating against you because you was out of Hungate.

Guy King-Reynolds describes his father.

Father was a local doctor and consequently most of these people in Hungate and Layerthorpe were what was then called his panel patients.

He was also police surgeon and I suppose one or two of them got to know him in other circumstances too, after a very good Saturday night. He did a lot of work with Seebohm Rowntree, who published that famous document on Poverty in York. And he did a lot of work because obviously he was seeing a great deal of real poverty. I can remember food parcels going out, and some of the children without shoes.

He was the first Labour Councillor for the Guildhall Ward of York, which was quite astonishing. He used to tell a funny story, of him standing as a Labour Councillor, and some of his patients, bless 'em, were as poor as church mice, and would come into his surgery and say, "Doctor you're not standing for Labour? Standing for the council's

Dr Reynolds' election pamphlet, 1929

great but not for Labour, doctor, not for Labour!" They expected him to
be Conservative but he was what you'd call an old-fashioned Labour.
He was just appalled by the poverty he was working under, which was
absolutely the antithesis of his father, who was a staunch Conservative
and was slightly horrified that his son was standing as a Labour man,
for which he was then duly elected as a councillor. In 1929 they won
Guildhall Ward for the first time in history. It had been Conservative
all the time.

The only time I remember father being attacked was when he was called
by the neighbours. In those days doctors were much more, sort of priests
as well, social workers. It was one Christmas Day and we were going
to sit down to Christmas dinner. A little child came to the door and
said, "Oh doctor will you come please, separate father and mother". He
stopped it and the wife turned on him, "You leave him alone". He was
called out three or four times a night, very often to drunks. In the old
days, in the police station was a notice on the wall. They could ask for
a bed and ask for a blanket, or ask to see a doctor, and this was on the
police wall in those days, and believe me they did get called out. And we
had one of those speaking tubes from the street. And he used to make 'em
walk a straight line and say things like, "Burgess's fish sauce shop".

And of course he used to be called out as police surgeon when they
fished bodies out of the river. I remember my father coming back,
somebody had been in the river for about six months and the policeman
said, "You'd better hold your nose doctor, it's a bit meller". I remember
father telling us that lovely story of people coming to see him with a
bad foot, for instance, and he would examine the foot and he said, "Take
off your other sock", and there'd be a horrified silence and, "I haven't
washed it". Yes, they'd washed the one foot and not the other one.
Again you've got to realise these are cold taps outside.

There was a lot of rickets though, and bow-legged kids. And with those
very high boots with a big heel, club feet. I mean there was medicine but

still it was, in terms of rectifying malformations, non-existent. If you were born like that well it was hard luck, you struggled.

And there was the workhouse too, which everyone dreaded. And that was a great shock, when they started talking about taking away the workhouse. You go in and could have a bath and breakfast, but you had to work, just break wood or something. But there was somewhere to go, now there isn't.

Poverty and the Community Spirit

The parish was very poor, yet the poverty and deprivation meant that people shared with each other, as they were 'all in the same boat'. The community fostered the spirit of mutual help and care, without much aid from outside. Institutions such as the church were supportive to an extent, but there were certain individuals who were genuinely concerned as Andy Waudby testifies.

You had Reverend Pyne doing what he could. And Dr Reynolds, Miss Ramsay and Mr Pickering. Now he had the bookshop in High Ousegate before the Shambles. He belonged to Centenary Chapel, that was in St Saviourgate. Now I had occasion to meet some of the people that went to Centenary Chapel, and they were so kind. Mr Pickering was such a wonderful chap. And I remember he used to come on a bike and take us for scouts.

Reverend Pyne of St Cuthbert's, he didn't wait for you to go to church, he brought the church to you. The bishops in their fine palaces and posh cars were nowhere to be seen when it meant practising Christianity. On a cold night we went to a small meeting house which belonged the Band of Hope. A nice warm hall with forms. Miss Ramsay gave us soup and sweets and we would say prayers and sing hymns. They'd teach us how to love and pray.

So through poverty and this suffering, they had this feeling for others, regardless of what colour you were. Now I went to school with Chinese sons. Now we accepted 'em straightaway, cos when you're living in poverty and hard times, you always have a feeling for your fellow man. This is why Hungate people and Walmgate people and Layerthorpe, they're wonderful people. They'll give you anything. Anybody knocked at the door and wanted a cup of tea or something to eat, we'd share it with 'em straight away. This is Hungate people. That makes us so proud. Because we feel for others.

They didn't all go to church but they were more God-fearing people lived there than there was in the rest of York. They believed in Jesus and believed in God. For all their roughness, by they could fight as well, the women, they might be rough and ready, they were tough women but inside were ticking hearts of gold. If we had people like that nowadays, what a wonderful world it would be.

John Waite also went to Centenary Chapel for cubs and scouts.

Donald Pickering who had Pickering's newsagent's shop in Ousegate at that time, [and later opened Pickering's bookshop in the Shambles], *was the scoutmaster, so we used to go there. That was very happy times. Quite a few of the Hungate people used to belong to the cubs and scouts and go camping. We used to go some weekends out to Stockton on Forest. At other times, Pickering would take us to his shop and he had one room upstairs that was laid out with an electric train. It was a display for his selling, but also I think he must have had a bit of a hobby with it, 'cos there was a lot of detail went in it.*

Lavinia Kay explains

There was a lot of poverty. And Reverend Pyne used to come round and he used to help, he helped everybody. He was a kind man. He saw that people didn't go hungry. If he thought that anybody was, he'd get other people to keep an eye on them, and if the neighbours say, "Well look these people are desperate", he would see they were all right. As far as he could.

If he thought you were desperate, he would give you the penny and you could get the old big white jug and off you went to the soup kitchen on Haymarket. That's where we went, me mum used to give us a penny and we'd take a big white jug, and she sent us off and well you could almost eat it with a knife and fork. It was so full of vegetables.

I had an aunt just lived across the road. We lived at number 5 and she lived across the road from us in this little street, and when she baked she'd stand at the door like this. "In here". "What?" "Never mind what, get in here". And she'd sit us down to a cup of tea and fresh baked bread. And that's how people were, everybody shared.

Rene Sheard also respected Mr Pyne.

He was a wonderful man, Reginald Pyne. He used to come in the pub when the men were enjoying their pints and chat away to them. He was no high up business because he was a vicar.

As well as being Rector of St Cuthbert's from 1910 to 1934, Rev Pyne was also president of the Racecourse Mission and the Railway Mission. When he died in February 1934, there was a huge turnout to line the streets for his funeral.

Samuel Thompson visited another soup kitchen in Dundas Street.

We used to go with a jug for two pennorth of soup. They all had big families, six or seven in a family. I was the middle one, there was six kids.

Everyone was willing to help in an emergency, in any practical way that they could, as Wally Holmes says.

If you wasn't doing any baking, next door neighbour would do it for you and you'd do her shopping. And you went in each other's houses helping 'em wash.

There was allus one person in t'street, if somebody was having a baby, they would be there to see it into the world. Or if somebody had died, there'd be somebody there to come into your house and lay 'em out for you.

Wally Holmes as a young man

Wally Holmes, 1995

Louisa Aldrich also remembers,

We had a food kitchen on Walmgate and we went there from school for our dinners, free dinners. We went down a passage and about half way down at left hand side. Beautiful an' all. There was loads went. And there was a soup kitchen on St Saviourgate itself.

There was a place down Lady Peckitt's Yard. We went down there and we got some boots what you lace up, and an odd coat or two, but we didn't get much because there were so many wanted them. Some went in their bare feet. They used to get cardboard or anything and make soles in their shoes, to hide the holes in the outer soles.

If you were lucky you got some things given. But sometimes you used to go errands for old people. And they would give you a penny or something like that, and you used to take it home to your mother, a penny was a lot in them days, and pay it towards helping your mother.

Alice Butterworth had the same experience.

I've gone without shoes and socks meself. Well I did once and I was in me bare feet and these people shouted of me. And I daren't stop so I just ran home. And when I told me mam, she said, "Yer soft cat, they might 'a been going to buy you some shoes".

I mean we were poor but we weren't that poor that me mam couldn't feed us. And we were always clean. But as I say, nothing posh. But I think our days were better than they are today somehow. I suppose our parents knew how to contrive better than what they do today.

The food that was available always went first to the head of the house, as Mr Thompson knew well.

My father used to get two boiled eggs for his tea on a Friday payday and we used to take it in turns to get the top of the egg. They would put veg and carrots and all sorts in to make soup, and that would last you two days. You got soup and that were it. Good old days!

George Squire stresses that the classes did not mix.

There was another pub on Dundas Street, where the first soup kitchen opened. Pea soup. You took a jug or a bowl. If you were poor, you were poor, if you were wealthy you were wealthy, and they never mixed. People in the houses in St Saviourgate never mixed with Hungate. No way.

John Waite was an exception. Although he lived in St Saviour's Place,

All my friends were Hungate people. I went to school with them, I went to their houses with 'em, I went on the Salvation Army trips to Filey with them, because we didn't have a lot of money. We used to go fishing with 'em, play with 'em all the time. Most of the St. Saviourgate people were grown up, there wasn't a lot of children down there.

If a person became really destitute then the final port of call was the workhouse, as Andy Waudby reflects.

I remember my granny taking in this poor lass. I can just picture her now, and nobody wanted her. My granny had a heart o' gold. My granny took her in for a time, but I don't know if she finished up in the workhouse. She'll have died. The workhouse people were on Huntington Road.

You could always tell a person who was from the workhouse because he had a grey suit. When he got too old and couldn't work anymore, he couldn't sit back and get money. He finished up in the workhouse and some of 'em used to stop there the night but they had to chop sticks before they got food.

The police took away men in strait-jackets who were broken down through despair. Men committed suicide by cutting their throats. Ex-soldiers with legs off, arms off, came round singing for pennies, or sold matches or bootlaces because they could not get work. These men had fought for their country and were promised by the idiots in

*Andy Waudby in
the army, 1939*

*Parliament that they would come back to a land fit for heroes to live
in. It certainly took a hero to live in it! There were men who were
breathless, could hardly walk, their lungs shattered by poisoned gas.
The wives queued outside the pawnshop on Monday mornings with
bed sheets or anything they could sell. First World War soldiers told me
how York local councillors urged men to join up and fight but after the
war they sat on parish boards cutting men's dole. They told old soldiers
to sell their furniture to get money. If you had a piano, your dole was
stopped and you were told to sell it. When I was poorly I had to go into
the infirmary, it was part of the workhouse. You had no money. I had
pneumonia in the workhouse.*

I was in the army. Now your blokes in Burma, biggest part of the blokes who were fighting were either coalminers or blokes out of t'slums. The conditions in the jungle were so bad, and you were fighting a tough enemy, the biggest part of your blokes come out of t'slums, all over the country, because they were the lads who could go up against the Japanese and fight. They were nigh on starving in the jungle. I had to go without food, that's why I have no muscles. We walked over swamps, jungles, over mountains. The army weren't bloody daft, picked lads from the slums.

Nell Fearn remembers the Depression when people were reduced to combing the streets to find food and cigarette ends.

The corner shop, Alf Huckle's, they used to congregate round there during the depression, did the men. We called 'em men, 17, 18, 19.

They were called balls in those days, the dances, and that's what they were. And there was the De Grey Rooms and Assembly Rooms. Lovely places now, but then they were all lit up and everything. They used to arrive there in all their evening clothes, the ladies and the men as well. We used to go just to stand and watch. See what clothes they had on. Especially the women. And the men used to go in maybe sections of three and they'd take whichever pitch they wanted there, outside the Assembly Rooms or the De Grey Rooms. And some of 'em used to go outside the Empire. But this was when these big dances were on. And they used to go for cigar ends. Butt ends of cigarettes. Stick with a pin or whatever it was. They used to put 'em in this tin. And I've watched 'em stood at top of that street the following day, and they used to share, they'd share what they had. That's how bad it was.

For some people there were alternative options, though these were not always regarded sympathetically as George Squire points out.

*They had no money but they had high morals. If a lass got pregnant she
was a whore, the illegitimate child was a bastard. The fellers could do
as they liked but a woman was either right or wrong, pure or otherwise.
There's one family and the daughter came down Hungate with a fur
coat on, and I was sat outside a shop. What a beautiful lass. Mickey
said, "Oh yes, she's doing well, she's come from working on Piccadilly".
I said, "Whereabouts in Piccadilly?" "Piccadilly in London. She's on
t'game". I couldn't balance it out. "What game?"*

Wally Holmes explains,

*As a community though, it was a civilisation killed when they moved it.
The people may look on us as poor people. We weren't poor at all. What
with character and everything else, we were rich. We was happy. I'll
stand on the rooftops and shout it, where I was born and where I was
fetched up.*

George Squire found that,

*The people were very caring, you didn't do anything wrong because
they didn't allow you to, they'd give you a clatter and put you right.
There was a lot of intertwining of people and families. They were all
very self-opinionated, all the families did well.*

*They were very sociable. They used to sit out in chairs in the evening
in summertime in the street, either knitting or talking across the street.
Old Granny Dodd used to nurse 'em all. It was a self-help community.*

James Cave agrees.

*If anybody died, some woman in the street would lay them out.
Everybody rallied round. No-one dreamed of opening the curtains,
always drew them when a funeral passed. On Sunday at St Saviour's
Church, loaves of bread were given out to poor parishioners. People*

149

gathered together without having to be asked, the feeling was marvellous.

May Greenley speaks of the same spirit of kindness in her mother.

A girl once came who'd been to St Andrewgate and had a baby in a field. No-one would take her in. Mum was good with people and took her in and she put her a bed on the floor. Next morning she'd gone and taken the blankets. Mother said, "Don't call t'police. She must have wanted them".

John Waite remembered Hungate even when he was on his travels.

They did pull together, very close in Hungate. I think living in the close conditions that they were more communal, they helped each other a lot. I've travelled quite a lot since then, and I've only ever seen it in third world countries. I was wandering in the back streets of Calcutta, and I looked and I thought, "Hungate". They had the same communal feeling there as in Hungate in those bygone days. I'm not saying that the way of life was good, the conditions that they were living under, they were certainly a lot better when they moved them out. But they lost a way of life once they split Hungate up.

Nell Fearn sums up the attitude of the Hungate community.

It was marvellous. Everybody helped everybody else. If your mother didn't appear for a full day, your neighbours would pull you up in the street and say, "Where's your mother?" And if you said, "She isn't very well", they'd come in and they'd bring bread cakes. You never used to lock your doors at all. Anybody had been in your house when you got back, you knew that they'd been in because there'd be a fruit pie on the table. It was to put something in, not to take something out.

If you lived in that area, I don't care where you went, anywhere in the world, I can honestly say, we looked after one another. You was never allowed to wander. But I mean if you was, everybody knew who you were. If you was out there when you was about eight or nine, they used to take you home. Things like what happen today could never have happened in those days, because you were watched over by every family.

It was a tough environment, but it wasn't a vicious environment compared to today's standard. These women were this type, you saw them stood at the street end talking, and obviously they always did, arms folded, sort of having a real good chinwag, and if there was anything matter with you at all, whether you'd fallen, cut yourself, or whether you was wet, miserable, for something that had gone on at home, you had open arms. You could go to 'em, everybody was either like your mother or your grandmother. You always felt safe. Always.

My mam died when she was early forties. And there was six of us left. And youngest was six months old, and me dad brought us all up. And by God, he got a lot of help. They couldn't do enough for you. I mean, anywhere he had to go for anything, the kids were looked after. And they didn't only take you and look after you, they did for you what you've got to pay babysitters to do now. They washed you and put you to bed, they had the run of the house, and you had the run of their house in return. And there was the Depression during this period that I'm talking about as well.

You had to share what you had down Hungate. It was a community and it would be a damn sight better today if there was a few more like it.

Picture Credits

Bibliography

Harris, A. "Chicory in Yorkshire". *Yorkshire Archaeological Journal.* Vol 59. 1987

Kelly's and White's Street Directories of York 1898-1950

Knight, C. B. *A History of the City of York.* Herald Printers 1944

Murray, Hugh. *A Directory of York Pubs 1455-2004.* Voyager 2004

Watson, A. G. (Ed). *York City Yearbook and Business Directory 1909-1930*

York City Council Maps of Hungate

York City Council Minutes 1935

York City Council Video. *Hungate – A Vanished Community*

York City Reference Library Newspaper Index

York Times. Vol 3. No 1. Early Spring 1963

Yorkshire Evening Press. 1908 and 1933

Books by the same Author

The History of a Community : Fulford Road District of York. College of Ripon & York St John 1984.

Alexina : A Woman in Wartime York. 1995

Rich in All But Money : Life in Hungate 1900-1938. York Archaeological Trust. 1996

Beyond the Postern Gate : A History of Fishergate and Fulford Road. York Archaeological Trust. 1996

Humour, Heartache and Hope : Life in Walmgate. York Archaeological Trust 1996

York Memories. Tempus Publishing 1998

Number 26 : The History of 26 St Saviourgate, York. Voyager 1999

Voices of St Paul's. Oral History of St Paul's Church (Edited). Sessions of York. 2001

Rhythm and Romance : An Oral History of Popular Music in York. Vol. 1 The Dance Band Years. York Oral History Society 2002

Something in the Air. An Oral History of Popular Music in York. Vol 2 The Beat Goes On. York Oral History Society 2002

The Walmgate Story. Voyager 2006

Acknowledgements

Grateful thanks go to the individuals and organisations who helped to fund the first edition of this book – Jack Birch, RM Burton Trust, Friends Central Adult School Trust, Scirebröc Group, Sheldon Memorial Trust, Julie Thompson, and York Common Good Trust. Thanks also go to the original photographer, Simon I Hill, formerly head of photography at York Archaeological Trust, and to Andrew 'Bone' Jones who conceived the original idea and set up the project ten years ago.

I would particularly like to thank the Garfield Weston Foundation for their funding of this new edition, Hugh Bayley, MP for York, for his introduction to the book, and York Oral History Society for allowing us the use of material and photographs.

I would also like to thank Sarah Maltby, Director of Attractions at York Archaeological Trust, and John Walker, Chief Executive, for the idea of revising this book, and for their support.

Special thanks to Lesley Collett, Graphics Officer at York Archaeological Trust, who has taken many of the modern photographs, copied the older photographs and designed the book itself; to Michael Andrews for the finds and excavation photographs, and to Christine Kyriacou, the Trust Archivist, for her involvement with this project, and for proof-reading the manuscript and making useful suggestions.